Social Media Strategies for Entrepreneurs

Wilma M. Ray

ABSTRACT

Social media has emerged as a formidable force in both synergistic engagement and economic influence, offering unprecedented strategic advantage across diverse business sectors. Particularly for small enterprises historically constrained by limited access to expansive marketing channels. Social media has facilitated transformative opportunities for visibility, outreach, and sustained growth in competitive markets. The importance of social media to the small business owner is significantly greater than that of the larger firms, which have greater customer reach and traditional marketing influence. The purpose of this qualitative exploratory multiple case study was to explore the perceptions of owners, employees, and customers on the influence of social media on microenterprise family-owned businesses in the Delaware, Maryland, and Virginia (DELMARVA) region. This study aimed to address the existing apertures within the current body of research. This research highlights and identifies the challenges that small business owners encountered and had to overcome concerning competitive pressure, IT infrastructure capabilities, organizational capabilities (marketing management and innovation management), and firm size in developing a social media competence. The research analysis in this paper suggests that microenterprise required some level of social media competence to expand their reach and become more competitive in the business market. This research also shows that social media competence was important for smaller firms in creating local consumer loyalty, repeat business, and increased profits.

Contents

Chapter 1

Introduction

With the growth of the World Wide Web, the implementation of social media products used by businesses as a marketing technique to provide the availability of goods and services to many customers has expanded since the 1990s (Bashir et al., 2020). The use of social media has become significantly more commonplace, accepted, and implemented by companies of all sizes. Al-Omoush et al. (2021) indicated that social media consumer acceptance and support of this technology are becoming critical components of all businesses, and with the advent of customer responses via online appbased ratings and comments, the use of social media becomes even more critical for small business owners. Microenterprises are the smallest of small businesses, with just 1-20 employees (Handayani, 2023). Although social media increasingly is becoming an essential consideration for these microenterprises, the best-fit social media approaches adopted by family-owned microenterprises are not yet well understood. This study was intended to understand what microenterprise owners encountered using social media.

Chapter 1 provides an introduction and overview of this study. Chapter 1 begins by discussing the background of the research problem. Then, the problem itself was developed, along with the corresponding research purpose. The study population and sample are addressed. The significance of the study is discussed, followed by the nature of the study. The research questions guiding the study are presented, along with the conceptual framework.

Chapter 1 concludes with key terms, assumptions, limitations, delimitations, and a summary.

Background of the Problem

The social media landscape in 2024 is interwoven into everyday personal interaction, is technically complex, and presents competitive challenges that every business leader must face (Agarwal & Puppala, 2024). The process of implementing and acting on decisions that determine the use of technologies that best benefit each organization, as Aichner et al. (2021) indicated, is critical to the success of that business. Bashir et al. (2020) suggested that small business owners in locations like Delaware, Maryland, and Virginia, or colloquially known as the DELMARVA region, compete for customers in this highly transient area, and need to approach the implementation of social media with a clear plan that was specific, measurable, achievable, relevant, and adaptable to the influences of this consumer base.

In connecting social media to consumer interaction during the mid-2020s, Treyz (2023) found that the economic and social migration in the DELMARVA region is part of the consumer engine that drives these local economies. This unique market segment consisting of U.S. military and the Federal Government directly or indirectly employs a sizable portion of the workforce in this region. This research focused on small familyowned businesses, or microenterprises, in this region, including surrounding rural market areas and the competition for these customers. Given consumers' ever-changing purchasing preferences, the research explored social media's influence on small businesses in the DELMARVA, more specifically the Baltimore region, (Son & Niehm, 2021).

Success in a social media environment includes benefits in attracting mobile consumers and providing one of the most critical elements in customer interaction negative or positive feedback from the customer (Dolega et al., 2021). Further, Dolega et al. (2021) indicated that the existing research addresses entrepreneurs' goals of implementing social media as a marketing tool. Yet, it was not clear that microenterprise owners fully understand social media usage in managing customer relationships. This want of information creates gaps in the data available to small business entrepreneurs (Dwivedi et al., 2021). This research study also examines consumer social media search patterns, but the research needs to focus more on business influences and the information available in 2024. Social media, as a technology-based tool, is constantly evolving and the providers and users of these tools need to stay informed and adapt to these changes.

The implementation of social media as a tool for business marketing is growing exponentially nationwide, substantially affecting business revenues (Dwivedi et al., 2023). There is a need for more current information on the successful marketing techniques of small business owners using social media in the DELMARVA region. Social media concepts and technology as marketing tools are moving and influencing business segments in many new and dynamic directions, and small business owners should be aware of the tidal movement (Luckman et al., 2020). These shifts may be of even greater relevance to extra small and microenterprises or those with twenty or fewer employees (Handayani, 2023). Many microenterprises have a social focus, making social media even more important for them (Aracil-Jordá et al., 2023) because microenterprises rely on a more personal experience, personal interaction efforts which social media can help them provide.

Small family business owners in this region look for ways to attract customers, improve cash flow, and remain competitive. Salloum et al. (2021) found that the acceptance and ease of use of social media applications and tools replace traditional advertising in locations like small towns and residential areas with a fluid customer base. Locations with large transient or fluid customer bases are usually not known for a dedicated number of consumers (Son & Niehm, 2021). As such, businesses in these areas need new ways to attract and retain customers even more than elsewhere. As Zhang et al. (2023) found, digital transformation has significant potential to sway corporate performance. A business decision to support and connect to consumers and social media marketing content is critical to the success of small businesses (Al-Qaysi et al., 2020). Small businesses' implementation of social media technologies allows consumers to use content to make daily purchasing decisions.

Innovative technologies, such as social media, often support the goals and objectives of small businesses and are highly effective, requiring lower investments than other forms of marketing. The lower marketing cost and social media use by businesses and consumers can directly sway customer decisions positively, but may also sway decisions potentially negatively, both decisions influencing company revenues and value (Dolega et al., 2021). However, implementing fresh, usable, and reliable consumerrelated content within the small company environment, as Gellweiler and Krishnamurthi (2020) indicated, takes resources, time, and effort.

Several technological and financial challenges exist for small business owners when reviewing the need for and implementing social media as a viable marketing technique. Small company owners must make a commitment that provides for a chance for success when implementing social media. First, small business owners must recognize, understand, and accept social media's growth and performance outcomes as viable marketing tools (Popescu & Tulbure, 2022). Second, owners must realize that social media technologies could significantly influence the payoff in brand recognition, business-to-business commerce, and the resulting company revenues, as Dwivedi et al. (2023) indicated, also resulting in company growth and consumer loyalty. This growth supports and expands the company's ability to remain competitive. Finally, committing to social media marketing instead of traditional media venues requires investment within the business and the owner understands that this technology should provide the returns on the investment the business owner seeks.

Problem Statement

The problem is microenterprise business owners and employees in highly transient regions may not possess strong business-related social media skills, resulting in challenges in creating successful customer-focused social media business strategies (Ahmad et al., 2021). Businesses in more transient areas have significantly higher competition for a limited customer base (Bashir et al., 2020). At the same time, because many microenterprises have social rather than financial focus (Aracil-Jordá et al., 2023), these businesses are even more susceptible to the pressures associated with doing business in a transient region. Social media offers potential competitive advantages for businesses trying to survive and thrive in highly competitive transient areas (Dolega et al., 2021). However, the specific reasons why these businesses adopt their social media strategies, the success of those strategies, and the challenges presented by those strategies remain poorly understood at present. Further research was needed on the use of social media by microenterprises in a more diverse array of unconventional contexts (Cheing et al., 2020). Further research was also needed regarding what tools and strategies are most effective for small businesses when using social media marketing (Popescu & Tulbure, 2022). In addition, research was needed to understand the drivers of social media usage more comprehensively among small businesses (Kwon et al., 2021).

Purpose of the Study

The purpose of this qualitative exploratory multiple case study was to explore the perceptions of owners, employees, and customers on the influence of social media on microenterprise family-owned businesses in the Delaware, Maryland, and Virginia (DELMARVA) region. The data collection for the research involved five distinct cases.

Business owners and employees from five microenterprises were recruited for the study. Owners participated in individual interviews or online instruments; employees also participated in an interview or online email instruments. In addition, contextualizing data was collected as a result from the interview and instrument processes that supplied context and richness to the data. The results of the study may provide beneficial information that supports improved performance for small or microenterprise type businesses.

Population and Sample

A study population represents the overall group the study intends to research (Banerjee & Chaudhury, 2010). In this case, the study population consisted of five microenterprise owners, employees, and business customers in the DELMARVA region or boundary. Microenterprises are the smallest category of small businesses, those with fewer than five employees (Handayani, 2023). The participant criteria required that the microenterprises be family-owned businesses with revenues of less than five million dollars, have five or less employees and specific to the area boundary.

The research focused on family-owned businesses in the DELMARVA area. This narrowly defined local business community needs more research into the use of social media as the information found was limited and needs more literature about using social media as a marketing tool. The research also included the processes the microenterprise owners used to implement social media technology, perceptions of the success or failure of the process, and ideas of the how and why of social media for the small business community.

Within this overall population of 1.5 million small businesses in the Tri-State area (see Figures 2, 3 and 4), the research focuses was on a target population that consisted of five family-owned microenterprise owners and employees in a highly transient DELMARVA region. The transience of the region was expected to play a significant role in the types of social media strategies used by microenterprises and their efficacy. Within this population, five specific microenterprises were selected as case study.

Participants were recruited using purposive criterion sampling, the criteria were based on small, family-owned microenterprises, having fewer than five employees and limited revenues to five million dollars. In purposive criterion sampling, participants were chosen for their relevance to answering the study research questions (Etikan et al., 2016). One owner and employee from each of the five businesses participated in an individual interview or completed the email instrument, and customers were provided online surveys to complete via SurveyMonkey. Each microenterprise fits into the current research study criteria.

The email instruments were completed by one employee from each of the five businesses. A request to engage one employee was made to the business owner, and was an employee that works during regular business hours. This employee could work at the front cash register or assist customers. The selection of that employee-type resulted in the ones that were most available for the research. The interview was not take more than 2030 minutes and was not meant to conflict with any regular business in which the employee may be engaged. Random customers were provided with QR scannable codes via a flyer at the point of sale and directed the customer towards an online survey, which was used to determine the impact social media might have had on the customers' decision to visit the store. The ability to select an employee and a customer was approved by the business owner. All consent paperwork and expressed confidentially with all participants, was maintained throughout the interviews.

Additional data from the businesses' social media pages and customer surveys were gathered. This data was captured through a perusal of social media pages such as Facebook and Twitter and a review of the business's web pages if, they had one. The expectation was that most of the business information had been captured through Facebook and neighborhood pages such as Nextdoor, an application that provides insight into local issues. These social media interfaces were reviewed for information that provided insight into the acceptability of the business in the community and for any feedback that supported or diminished that acceptability.

Significance of the Study

This study has significance from both theoretical and practical standpoints. From a theoretical standpoint, the study recognizes a lack in the literature. This gap was highlighted by prior calls for research. Firstly, Cheing et al. (2020) studied social media use by microenterprises. Although their results emphasized the importance of social media to such businesses, the scope of their study was highly constrained, and Cheing et al. (2020) called for more research on the topic in a more diverse array of unconventional contexts. This research study explores the questions of social media use within a transient population, which may be considered unconventional for microenterprises.

Popescu and Tulbure (2022) wrote about the general importance of social media to small businesses, calling for additional research on what tools and strategies are most effective for small businesses when using social media marketing. Looking at microenterprises specifically, by interviewing both owners and employees, this study provided valuable insights about the various strategies used by small businesses. These strategies also provided visibility into successful or unsuccessful deployments of social media platforms. These platforms could prove to be the pivotal part of a competitive, thriving establishment.

Kwon et al. (2021) studied internal and external drivers of social media use by small businesses. However, Kwon et al. (2021) results were limited to a single driver of external and internal use, and they called for research to understand the drivers of social media usage more comprehensively among small businesses. The research study explored the perceptions of the owners of microenterprises and their employees concerning the need for, and the use of social media for personal and business use.

This study also has practical significance. The importance of social media for small businesses was well-established (Popescu & Tulbure, 2022). However, microenterprises are a specific class of small businesses that have seen less focus on social media use. Many microenterprises, especially those run by women, who may be less financially focused than other small businesses (Aracil-Jordá et al., 2023). The importance of social media, yet the lack of focus on its use, makes understanding the strategies that can be used by these microenterprise mall businesses to succeed especially important because they are more likely to struggle.

Small-to-medium enterprises (SMEs) are the main drivers of job creation in the economy (Gherghina et al., 2020). Additionally, microenterprises represent an essential and formative segment of the SME market (Handayani, 2023). Hence, improving microenterprises' performance through better social media marketing can improve the overall economy.

Nature of The Study

The research methodology used in this research was a qualitative exploratory multiple case study. Qualitative research was an open-ended and exploratory research approach (Merriam & Tisdell, 2015). A qualitative study was used to explore the perceptions of key population groups that are of interest to a researcher (Liamputtong, 2020). Because of its open-ended nature, qualitative research was ideal for exploring latest ideas (Merriam & Tisdell, 2015).

Qualitative research was appropriate to this study for several reasons. First, this research was intended to explore and describe the social media strategies used by microenterprises. Secondly, the purpose purpose of this qualitative exploratory multiple case study was to explore the perceptions of owners, employees, and customers on the influence of social media on microenterprise family-owned businesses in the Delaware, Maryland, and

Virginia, (DELMARVA) region.. Thirdly, the topic of this research was relatively new, making preliminary qualitative exploration necessary.

The specific qualitative research design has been a multiple case study. Case study research is contextual in nature (Yin, 2017). A case study researcher focuses on one or more specific cases of the general phenomenon and explores them thoroughly *in situ,* or place of origin (Stake, 2008). Case study also offers a rich depiction of reality with multiple data sources (Yin, 2017).

A case study design was appropriate to this study foremost because following Yin (2017), the study was contextual. The research was focused on microenterprises specifically located in this transient area, giving the study a contextual focus. In addition, the study benefited from multiple data sources, which then allowed for the exploration of social media marketing strategies from multiple perspectives within different micro entrepreneurial organizations. Therefore, the research approach was exploratory multiple case study because the study and was intended to explore new theoretical ground. In an exploratory case study, the researcher seeks to conduct a preliminary exploration of a novel topic (Stake, 2008). This research provided much needed information from more than one business perspective in a specific region and provided some level of insight into developing social media strategies for microenterprises and SMEs in the future.

An alternative design would have been phenomenology. Phenomenology involves in-depth exploration of the participants lived experiences (Moustakas, 1994). This study, however, was concerned with understanding broader strategies and results, not specific experiences. Another option would have been grounded theory. Grounded theory involves developing or verifying a new theory from the raw data (Strauss & Corbin, 1997). This study, however, already has a theoretical framework and therefore does not require a grounded theory approach.

Data collection for the study involved multiple data sources from each of the five businesses that were the subjects of the proposal. Of the five business owners, all five business owners completed online email instruments. Additionally, all the five employees from each business completed an online email instrument as well. For customers, an online survey was provided at each business location, via a flyer posted, and could be completed using a QR code or web link. This provided the customers some level of flexibility in completing the survey when practicable. A perusal of the website for each business was also conducted to review comments directly related to the business, but that data was only used as a secondary data point as the owner's comments may be difficult to trace, as social media pages are public domain. Permission to interview business customers, employees, and owners was requested and obtained, and the confidentiality of all interviewees was ensured and always maintained. Data analysis involved triangulation and used Braun and Clarke's (2022) six-step qualitative thematic analysis.

Research Questions

The research was structured around the following three qualitative research questions, which served as the foundational framework guiding the inquiry:

R1: What are the owner perceptions at family-owned microenterprises in the DELMARVA region regarding their reasons for implementing social media strategies?

R2: What are the employee perceptions at family-owned microenterprises in the DELMARVA region regarding the influence with customers concerning business social media strategies?

R3: What are the customer perceptions at family-owned microenterprises in the DELMARVA region regarding accuracy and usability of the social media interfaces?

Conceptual Framework

The conceptual framework for the study combined the Business Model Innovation (BMI) concept (Gassmann et al., 2016) and Porter's theory of competitive advantage. Foss and Saebi (2017) defined business model innovation as "designed, novel, nontrivial changes to the key elements of a firm's business model and/or the architecture linking these elements" (p. 2). The BMI paradigm is a conceptual understanding of business models that intends to holistically integrate the key components of the business model itself and the ways in which firms make structured, nontrivial changes to their overall strategy or model (Gassmann et al., 2016). BMI applied to this study in the adoption of social media and social media-driven business strategies represents a significant business model innovation, especially for family-owned microenterprises.

Porter (1985) found that a company would excel if a business held a competitive advantage compared to its rivals. Porter's theory builds consumer and competitive advantage on captured data that illustrates social media's use and benefits as a replacement technology for traditional marketing within small family-owned businesses. Further, Manzoor et al. (2020) indicated that organizational management's adoption of social networking sites is linked to business profitability and long-term success.

Some theoretical concepts surrounding social media implementation included value, company loyalty, financial benefits, and technology deployment, underpinning small businesses' challenges in transitioning from traditional to social media marketing. As Krishen et al. (2021) indicated, many social media platforms support adopting digital marketing to engage consumers. The potential consumer can interface with social media marketing sites such as Amazon marketplace, eBay, Twitter, and Facebook, offering the small business owner many avenues to engage with potential customers. As such, effective use of social media represents a significant and potential source of competitive advantages.

Definition of Terms

Family-owned: A commercial organization is controlled by a family related by blood, marriage, or adoption and is that organization's primary shareholder and influencer

(Soluk & Kammerlander, 2021).

Microenterprise: A Microenterprise represents a business with 1-20 total employees (Handayani, 2023).

Small-to-medium enterprise (SME): A business employing fewer than 250 people (Cotrino et al., 2020).

Social Media: A network of electronic tools built on Web 2.0 that enables and supports making connections. (Egüz, 2020).

Social Media Marketing (SMM): A form of Internet marketing that utilizes social networking websites as a marketing tool. SMM aims to produce content that users will share with their social network to help a company increase brand exposure and broaden customer reach. (Evans et al., 2021).

Social Network: It is a web-based service where people connect with friends and acquaintances, enabling individuals to construct publicly accessible profiles and exercise discretion in curating their network of interpersonal connections. (Newman & Park, 2003).

Social Selling: Social selling represents the advantage of social communication to engage with prospects by answering questions and providing helpful content. (Newman & Park, 2003).

Transient: The customers' purchasing perspective and influence, or importance of the goods or services, ultimately affect their online shopping involvement. (Rubin et al.,

2020).

Assumptions, Limitations, and Delimitations

In research, assumptions, limitations, and delimitations play crucial roles in framing the study and carefully considering the scope and constraints (Bernard, 2025). Assumptions are underlying beliefs taken as true without verification, which form the foundation of the research; for instance, assuming that survey respondents will answer truthfully. Limitations refer to potential weaknesses or constraints in the study that are beyond the researcher's control, such as a limited sample size, time available, response bias, or data collection challenges, which may impact the generalizability of the findings.

Delimitations, on the other hand, are boundaries intentionally set by the researcher to narrow the scope of the study, like focusing on a specific geographic area or demographic group, to maintain manageability and relevance (Bloomberg et al., 2019). Understanding and clearly stating these elements ensures that the research was contextualized, and the findings are interpreted within a defined framework, acknowledging the study inherent constraint.

Assumptions

> Assumptions are the foundational components of a study that cannot be tested

(Liamputtong, 2020). Because these aspects are both foundational and untestable, they must be assumed to hold. There are assumptions underlying all research, including this study.

The first assumption was that family-owned microenterprises use social media to a significant degree. This assumption has basis in existing literature (Al-Omoush et al., 2021). Second, it was assumed that the participants will respond completely and accurately in the data collection, and that qualitative research with these microenterprises has been the optimal way to gain the information needed to address the research problem. The second assumption was needed because the study was qualitative and thus can only rely on the participants as its main source of data. Third, it was assumed that five familyowned microenterprises are willing to participate in this study. The third assumption was based on the high number of microenterprises in the area of interest.

Limitations

Limitations are the weaknesses or shortcomings inherent in a study (Merriam & Tisdell, 2015). Limitations come from the chosen methodology and therefore cannot be avoided. The following limitations are present in this research study. First, this research was limited by participants' self-reported data. When conducting a qualitative exploratory multiple case study, a researcher must rely on the participants to provide full and accurate answers to the interview questions. Respondents' answers limit the generalizability of results, as interview responses apply to the group studied, as quantitative research was not generalized.

Second, the study may be limited by social desirability bias. Social desirability bias reflects the tendency of participants to answer in ways that reflect well on the participants rather than to answer truthfully (Elston, 2021).

Third, this research was limited by self-selection bias. In self-selection bias, those who opt to participate may be materially different from those who do not (Elston, 2021). The transience of the region was expected to play a significant role in the types of social media strategies used by microenterprises and their efficacy. A fourth limitation may be the geographical boundary for the study. The DELMARVA region has a significant level of transitory businesses. The potential for microenterprise businesses in the region to use social media may be limited.

Available time to complete the study as time constraints represent a critical consideration in the administration of email-based survey instruments, particularly when seeking participation from respondents with professional or academic commitments. A researcher must balance the need for timely data collection with realistic allowances for participant engagement, ensuring that the allotted time is sufficient to foster thoughtful and complete responses.

Delimitations

Delimitations are the deliberately imposed boundaries of a study (Liamputtong, 2020). Delimitations are chosen deliberately to ensure that the study was fully focused and achievable. This study was delimited in the following ways. First, the study was delimited to microenterprises because of the research gap. Second, the study was delimited to social media because of the increasing importance of social media for advertising in the modern era. Third, the study was delimited to the DELMARVA region because of the researcher's interest in that region.

Chapter Summary

In summary, the problem was that it was not known how family-owned microenterprises in a highly transient area can implement effective social media marketing to promote their businesses. To address this problem, the purpose of this qualitative exploratory multiple case study was to explore the perceptions of owners, employees, and customers on the influence of social media on microenterprise familyowned businesses in the Delaware, Maryland, and Virginia (DELMARVA) region. This study was guided by three research questions: (a) What are the perceptions of owners and employees at family-owned microenterprises in the DELMARVA region regarding their reasons for implementing social media strategies? (b) What are the employees' perceptions at family-owned microenterprises in the DELMARVA region regarding the influence on customers concerning the business's social media strategies? and (c) What are the customers' perceptions of family-owned microenterprises in the DELMARVA region regarding the accuracy and usability of the social media interfaces? Chapter 1 offered an introduction to and overview of the study. In Chapter 2, the literature underlying this research was reviewed in depth.

Chapter 2

Review

Chapter 1 provided a comprehensive overview of small businesses' challenges while implementing and using social media and providing a competitive advantage. In addition, an overall description and purpose associated with the problem of deployment, use, and acceptance of social media as a replacement for traditional forms of advertising was presented (Dolega et al., 2021). This qualitative exploratory multiple case study, focused on the advantages and challenges of implementing and using social media for small businesses in the DELMARVA region and a review of the relatively small amount of empirical informational research offering insight into its use in this region.

In one study, Möhlmannn et al. (2023) indicated how managers conceptualize and use social media, identifying four distinct mindsets about business and customer interactions: business-to-customers, business-from-customers, business-with-customers, and business-for-customers. Looking further into the literature, Chapter 2 provides a review of the literature relating to the use of social media by small businesses within the geographical area surrounding the DELMARVA region, and more specifically the

Baltimore, Maryland area.

The focus of the literature review on social media and small business use has been to examine, understand, and analyze the existing research, as Dwivedi et al. (2021, 2023) found, and explore the realm of social media review, implementation, challenges, and use, specifically in the southern DELMARVA region. The literature review was designed to thoroughly understand the current state of knowledge on how small businesses engage with and leverage social media platforms through the study and analysis of information dated within the last five years from existing academic articles, books, and relevant publications. This research also explored the various strategies employed by small businesses, the impact of social media on marketing and customer relations, challenges faced, and potential opportunities identified.

Title Searches and Documentation

Title searches are executed using the University of Phoenix online library, ProQuest, EBSCOhost, Emerald, Small Business Administration Office of Advocacy, and Sage while utilizing Google, Google Scholar, and Yahoo web search engines. The searches served as the initial steps of the literature review, allowing the identification of relevant publications and establish a foundation for the literature review. The researched documents provided a broader understanding of overarching trends, challenges, and opportunities in the context of small family-owned businesses, specifically social media use as a technology. These sources contributed to a nuanced exploration of the multifaceted dynamics between social media platforms and small businesses. However, the specific regional topic of small business use within the DELMARVA region and the transient nature of consumers in this region tended to yield an even smaller research pool to review.

The literature search on small, microenterprise businesses utilizing social media highlighted the transformative impact of digital platforms on entrepreneurial strategies and market dynamics. This research emphasizes, as Daemi et al. (2021) found, the importance of understanding the unique challenges small businesses face, such as limited resources and expertise, in navigating the complexities of the digital landscape. The literature review highlighted the dynamic interplay between social media utilization and the connection to small business success, providing a foundation for further investigation into the context-specific dynamics, such as those within the small business landscape of the DELMARVA region.

After extensive research concerning the challenge of retaining customers using social media in the DELMARVA region, and more specifically the Baltimore area, more literature concerning this precise idea was needed. There needs to be more research material, as Wilson and Anagnostopoulos (2021) found, within the many literature databases examined concerning the small family-owned businesses, creating a research gap that the information in this paper may support. There is, however, significant information on social media's inclusion into the everyday lives of millions of people worldwide, with the advent of Amazon and other online shopping venues taking the place of in-person, brick-and-mortar shopping experience.

Using the literature available to examine the transition from traditional methods of consumer capture, or grabbing customer attention, to newer social media methods was difficult and complex to find but did serve a purpose. The transition was one that many small businesses are pursuing to stay competitive and build their customer base, as Paparini et al. (2020) found where the valuation of businesses was concerned. Given the transient nature of consumers in this specific area, which was of utmost importance. The existing research into the small business environment involving social media included several geographical regions.

It should be noted that significant gaps in data and information, as Li and Cho (2023) indicated, were discovered while searching these databases and journals for relevant topical texts specific to this subject matter and location. For example, social media implementation and use were limited and germane to the Baltimore region and, more specifically, to small businesses. However, many texts relating to social media were found dating from 2019 forward. Some of this data was relevant, but a considerable number were not.

Keywords identified for the research include *Social Media, Small Businesses, Information Systems, and Social Media Marketing*, with columns arranged with numbers of informational articles found. A significant amount of information was located in each search location, as social media has grown significantly in popularity. With the expansion and creation of different social media platforms, changes in leadership at those companies and how applications are used, the breadth of available information has also grown as Li and Cho (2023) indicated.

A high-level overview of the search properties used for literature research was provided in the research. Keywords were used to crawl the internet using search engines such as Google Scholar, Yahoo, Bing, and MS

Explorer. Searches included online databases searches, articles, journals, and internet searches. There are significant amounts of information on the internet concerning social media in its many forms, from business to political, from direct and live content to fake news. This research focused on business related and peer reviewed data directly concerning the subject matter. It should be noted that the number of databases, journals, and internet searches for this subject within a given period was constantly changing and extensive (Krishen et al., 2021). Several, but not all, articles and journals were read, and information about social media concerning small businesses was perused. Table 1 provides a list of data sources relevant to the research on the topic of social media. The online peer reviewed articles and databases in Table 1 included, the Small Business Administration, SAGE Journals, EBSCOhost, smallbusinessdb.com, ProQuest databases, and the University Library.

Table 1

Title Searches

Source Types	Social Media & Social Media Marketing	Small Business	Information Systems
Peer Reviewed Journal Articles	43	27	21
Books	10	7	4
Online Sources	5	5	3
Government Sources	2	0	3
Other	2	0	0
Total	62	39	31

Note. Table 1 provides the total number of articles and data found (Wieland, 2024)

Searchable business databases for small or microenterprise include ones from the Small Business Administration or SBA, the Delaware Division of Small Business provided by Delaware.gov, the Commerce Research Library provided by the Department of Commerce, Maryland and Virginia state websites, and Dun & Bradstreet. These databases provide lists of small, or microenterprises located in the DELMARVA region and the information available that relates to those businesses.

Historical Content

Three major developments starting in the 1960s have led to the creation of social media. In 1969, ARPANET was developed. McQuillan and Walden (1977) indicated the

Advanced Research Projects Agency (ARPA), a U.S. government agency, created ARPANET. ARPANET was an early network of time-sharing computers that formed the basis of the Internet. CompuServe, the third development of the 1960s, was also created in 1969 to provide corporations with time-sharing services by renting time on its computers.

The advent of email through intranet services, as Alford and Page (2018) indicates, occurred during the 1960s. The modern digital environment and email was originally a method of exchanging messages, or performing a check-in, as Alford and Page (2018) indicates, from one computer to another, but both computers were required to be online. However, the commercial Internet was not available to the public until 1991.

In the late 1980s, Vinton Cerf and others within the Defense Advance Research Project Agency (DARPA) built the initial foundational large-scale internet protocols that led to packet-based commercial online products, including the World Wide Web Crawler (Edosomwan et al., 2011). The development of internet technologies, from browsers to security, computing power to intelligence, has technically advanced significantly over the years.

Initially, because of extremely high fees, internet-provided services tended to be too expensive for many (Edosomwan et al., 2011). Bulletin boards (or BBS), systems were the predecessors of the World Wide Web.

Usenet, similar to a BBS which represented a foundational paradigm in digital communication, enabling asynchronous, text-based interactions and file exchanges among users via dial-up modems, thus laying critical groundwork for the evolution of contemporary online social networks, was conceived in 1979 and established in 1980. Usenet was a system to post articles or news. ThirdVoice and Napster were two examples of the original free file sharing software applications created in the 1990s that have since been removed from the market. ThirdVoice was a free plug-in that allowed users to post comments on web pages. There have been several new applications that have taken the place of these early forms of file and content sharing. User and customer communication, including feedback on business websites to provide insight and assurance of product or services reliability, were in the very early stages of social media development. There was much more to come.

Early Social Media

Early social media sites include Napster, a software application that allowed peerto-peer file sharing and a social media content-sharing community (Edosomwan et al., 2011). Users were allowed to share music files bypassing standard distribution methods, which were subsequently determined in 2001 to violate copyright laws. MySpace was one of the first social media applications. MySpace distributed content starting in 1997, leading to the initial thrust of this technology to provide a method for human interaction with other connected users informally and interactively. MySpace was one of the original user-driven social media search products that provided microblog and interest searches, creating consumer interest surrounding specific products and services.

In 2006, MySpace became the most popular social networking website in the United States but was overtaken by its competitor, Facebook, in 2008. Facebook (now Meta), launched in February 2004 and has grown to behemoth proportions. As Billore and Sadh (2015) indicates, the digital landscape is ever-changing. YouTube, another significant social media player, founded in 2005, is the world's most popular online video community, where millions of people can discover, watch, and share created videos.

The benefits of using websites and social media include increased awareness and inquiries, the internet was changing the way people interacted by providing not only information but also recommendations, reviews, and sales. The growth of this online culture has made having a website a significant advantage. Jones et al. (2015) indicated enhanced customer relationships, and an increased number of new customers emerged from social media sources. In the 2000s, social media soon became essential for all businesses, allowing business owners to communicate with, listen to, and learn from their customers in new and novel ways they never had before.

Focusing on entrepreneurial businesses in West London, UK, as Harris and Rae (2009) indicated, social networks played a vital role in the future of marketing. Harris and Rae found that externally, social networks used in businesses could replace customer annoyance with engagement. Internally, social networking helped to transform the traditional focus on control with an open and collaborative approach that was more conducive to success in the modern business environment.

Social media started to grow in the 2000s; Karimi and Naghibi (2015) found that social networks such as Facebook, Myspace, and LinkedIn; micro-blogs like Twitter, Plurk, and Friend Feed; and reviews and rating sites such as Yelp, Amazon, and Trip Advisor created a more engaged consumer. Video sites, such as YouTube and Vimeo, established more timely and direct communication processes at relatively low cost and higher levels of efficiency. Social media started to play a vital role in marketing and creating customer relationships.

Early on, it was found that social media technology held enormous potential for companies to become more connected to clients, as Kaplan (2015) found. Social media business use has been found to increase revenue, reduce costs, and improve efficiency. Facilitating conversations between sales and consumers using social media and building a critical relationship created opportunities for strategic usage by a business organization.

Social media platforms continued to emerge in the early 2000s, with the likes of Friendster laying the groundwork for online social interaction. However, Facebook's launch in 2004 marked a transformative moment by introducing a comprehensive and user-friendly platform that attracted a massive global user base (Karimi & Naghibi, 2015). The historical narrative was punctuated by key moments, such as the rise of usergenerated content, microblogging, and the explosive growth of visual-centric platforms.

During that time, social media became the enormous and synergistic economic powerhouse it has grown to today, providing an unforeseen advantage to small businesses that were not previously available. Snapchat, Facebook, YouTube, Yelp, Instagram, and Twitter are highly impactful social media platforms, as Kaplan (2015) found, influencing the daily lives of millions.

Extensive and strategic use of social media in the small business environment was still a novel concept. As Jones et al. (2015) found, small businesses' extensive strategic use of social media was becoming more prevalent as technology presents the potential to change consumer information processing and purchasing attitudes completely. Small business owners may subjectively and instinctively understand both the need for, and benefits of social media and the positive results technology could have on brand recognition and the business landscape. The purpose of this qualitative exploratory multiple case study was to explore the perceptions of owners, employees, and customers on the influence of social media on microenterprise family-owned businesses in the Delaware, Maryland, and Virginia (DELMARVA) region.

The importance of social media to small business owners should be greater than that of larger firms, which have greater customer reach and marketing influence and have potentially earlier adoption into the social media marketing process. Jones et al. (2015) found that social media's marketing potential to the small business community was significant. Given the competitive environment of small businesses in the DELMARVA region, differentiating the business using social media could mean the difference between business success and failure. Microenterprise business owners started to understand the importance of social media.

Internet and Traditional Marketing

The success or failure of small businesses often depends on favorable social media ratings, whereas in prior years, word of mouth may have taken many months; now, negative impacts for businesses are almost instantaneous. Large business owners and CEOs learned early in the 2000s to implement and use social media, which incentivized more extraordinary innovations (Harris & Rae, 2009). In addition, Harris and Rae (2009) found that the use of social media was becoming more commonplace as a marketing strategy by companies such as Amazon, Mobile, and IBM.

The intersection of small business strategies in social media, the Internet, and traditional marketing constitutes a dynamic and evolving landscape that has garnered significant attention. The original process of implementing social media or social networking as a marketing solution, as Edosomwan et al. (2011) indicated, revolved around bulletin boards, Usenet, and email applications, but quickly grew to blog applications and solutions that are more sophisticated.

Business Adjustment

Social media is self-evident as a global, impactful technology for large and small businesses, but this research focused on small businesses in the DELMARVA region, and more specially the Baltimore, Maryland area. From a historical perspective, social media was constantly changing, as Hogan and Quan-Haase (2010) found, and the successes or failures of companies utilizing this technology need to be reflected; that is, viewing the large success models of companies such as Amazon and Facebook may be different from the challenges small businesses encounter. Large companies have extensive resources to commit to innovative technologies that provide perceived value that many smaller companies still need. There was an interesting comparison on the impacts of negative reviews on microenterprises versus larger businesses.

Current Content

Social media as a tool and method for businesses to conduct marketing is growing exponentially. This has been shown to substantially affect business revenues (Dwivedi et al., 2023). The potential payoff in brand recognition, business-to-business commerce, and company revenues could be momentously influenced by social interaction, as Dwivedi et al. (2023) indicated, resulting in more significant company growth, consumer growth, and consumer loyalty. In searching for current content on social media, some particular keywords were used along with company information.

As Nyagadza (2020) found, conducting a thorough company search involves verifying the chosen business name's or brand's availability and uniqueness across various social media channels. Informational searches that provide title and name searches and detailed documentation collectively contribute to small businesses' effective and legally sound use of social media, helping them establish a solid online presence and navigate the complexities of the digital landscape.

Social Media

As a technology, social media significantly influences everyday life, including interests unrelated to the small business environment, such as political, financial, and personal interests (Wang et al., 2020). This social media research has specific focused on the interactions of social media applications, the impacts that technology has on small businesses, as indicated by Nyagadza (2020), and the challenges each business owner goes through in implementing the technology. Filtering social media through all the many entries within the searched information sources and focusing on the primary interest of small businesses within a specific location was no small feat. The goal of the research was, in fact, the use of social media by small businesses to attract consumers who live in a transient area.

Quansah and Hartz (2021) found that social media has revolutionized how small businesses connect with their target audiences, fostering unprecedented engagement and brand visibility opportunities. With the impact of applications like Facebook, Instagram, and Twitter, as indicated by Olson et al, (2021), companies can directly interact with customers, share compelling business content, and build a brand and a loyal community. Small businesses must conduct and understand their consumer base to secure a unique and recognizable online identity and create detailed documents of their social media activities to provide historical information.

Business owners generally understand that social media was a tool that can help them achieve competitive advantages and those investing in social media, go through a planning process to accomplish that goal (Abdulwase et al., 2020). By establishing a solid and engaging presence on platforms such as Facebook, Instagram, Twitter, and LinkedIn, as indicated by Olson et al. (2021), businesses can directly connect with their target audience, foster brand loyalty, and expand their customer base. Through strategic business-focused content creation and regular customer interactions, microenterprises can display their unique selling points, highlight customer testimonials, and effectively communicate their value proposition through social media. Social media also provides a cost-effective avenue for targeted advertising, enabling small businesses to reach specific demographics and optimize their marketing budgets.

As a focus for the small business marketing strategy, as Lupo and Stroman (2020) indicated, a well-crafted social media design empowers small businesses to survive and thrive, standing out amidst competitors and gaining a competitive edge in the digital landscape. Small businesses can strengthen their visibility and gain customer loyalty by actively participating in conversations, responding to customer inquiries, and utilizing specific, targeted social media advertising. A well-designed and thoughtful social media strategy helps small businesses establish a solid digital footprint, as indicated by Krishen (2021), and cultivates meaningful relationships with customers.

The understanding and development of social media as a marketing method and technology is one that each small business owner must understand before implementing it (Manzoor et al., 2020). This engagement process goes through stages of understanding the need to improve competitiveness, deciphering the digital landscape of different social media options, deciding, and implementing the marketing solution, and finally, observing consumer and customer responses. During this process, the owner should adapt and improvise to stay focused on the business goals and objectives and keep up with social media platform trends.

The literature surrounding social media, an instrumental resource for small businesses aiming to work the digital space effectively, was significant. This literature and library of work encompasses several topics, as indicated by Kaplan (2021), ranging from strategic marketing techniques to the intricacies of community management and online engagement. With the rapid growth of social platforms, understanding the nuances of effective communication, content creation, and brand positioning within these digital realms was imperative for businesses seeking to cultivate a robust online presence and connect meaningfully with their target audiences. Through diligent study and implementation of insights gleaned from this literature, enterprises can harness the power of social media as a dynamic tool for brand promotion, customer engagement, and organizational growth.

Figure 1 provides a general outline of the process that small business owners have gone through when considering the approach to social media implementation (Aichner et al., 2021). The marketing decision-making process was examined during the field test phase of the study, including all reviewed and historical information. Strategic agility and an emphasis on relationship-based marketing further distinguish the decision process, as microenterprises should continuously recalibrate their approaches to maintain competitiveness and foster sustainable growth within niche market segments. Figure 1 provides a rough draft of the process and procedures that the typical small business owner should consider, as Aichner et al. (2021) indicated when reviewing a change in marketing plans from traditional paper-based marketing to a digital space.

Figure 1

Social Media Small Business Decision Matrix

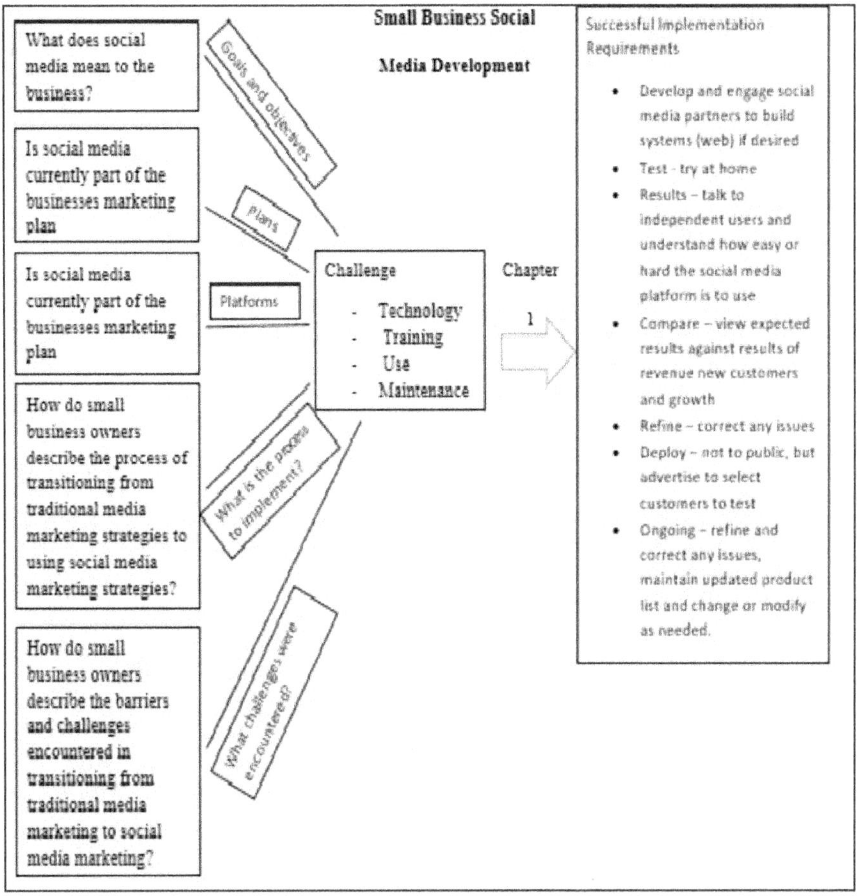

Note. Figure 1 describes a typical decision process for business when implementing social media tools (Wieland, 2024).

Small Business

For this research study, small business has been defined using the Small Business Administration definition, understanding that several factors contribute to calculating company size. As defined by the Small Business Administration (SBA), a small business is independently owned and operated, is organized for profit, and is not dominant in its field. Some business indicators in this market sector include the company's principal industry, the North American Industry Classification System (NAICS) codes, revenues, and economic factors. However, it was generally understood to have revenues ranging between 1 and 140 million US dollars and several full-time employees.

Competition in the Industry

In the dynamic landscape of contemporary commerce, small businesses are leveraging the power of social media to engage in fierce yet fruitful competition (Kahupi et al., 2021). The digital arena provides a level playing field for enterprises of all sizes, enabling small businesses to highlight their products and services alongside industry giants. Social media platforms like Facebook, Instagram, and Twitter serve as costeffective marketing and brand-building channels, allowing small businesses to reach a vast audience without hefty advertising budgets. The ability to connect with potential customers in real-time fosters community, loyalty, and trust, giving small enterprises a competitive edge. Through astute social media management, small businesses can survive and thrive, establishing themselves as formidable contenders in today's highly competitive business landscape.

Competition within social media for small businesses is increasingly fierce as enterprises strive to carve out their digital presence and engage with audiences meaningfully (Kahupi et al., 2021). Small enterprises often compete intensely for visibility, user engagement, and market share, necessitating strategic approaches to content creation, community building, and customer interaction. Small business owners generally understand they must tailor their content to their target audience and consistently adapt their strategies based on real-time analytics, customer feedback, and online messaging, depending on the method of social media used to support growth expectations. The competitive landscape in social media for small businesses underscores the significance of agility, creativity, and a keen understanding of the ever-evolving digital ecosystem.

Given the small business environment in the DELMARVA region and the transient nature of a sizable number of consumers within the military and government spectrums, the ability to differentiate one business from its competition creates a competitive advantage. Social media acts as a consumer multiplier, where word of mouth or customers passing opinions or referrals to friends, family, and others, was a different process of expanding the customer base. Medici (2023) found that social media stood out, with companies in this region joining buzz platforms like TikTok.

A primary goal of the research was to understand, from the business owner's perspective, through qualitative research, the success, or failures that social media brings to the small business environment. The research process included a review of perceptions of how impactful social media was for the microenterprise, and how social media was used from the vantage point of owners, employees, and customers. The research included how the technology was used and how the owners implemented social media to create a competitive advantage.

This exploratory case study reviewed the significant challenges to implementing and maintaining a social media presence, which gets even more different when monetary exchanges are included in the process. Depending on the level of implementation complexity, the small business owner wishing to engage with social media technology must determine, for the most part, the level of effort required to implement it. The amount of historical and relevant information available for the small business owner in this research area seems limited to what commercial social media companies offer.

There was a significant amount of information and sources, as Bawden and Robinson (2020) found, concerning the use of social media within medium to large business communities. However, the availability of data for research concerning smaller businesses was significantly limited, as indicated by (Olsson & Bernhard, 2021). The requirements in resources, time, and effort to implement and maintain a social media presence for small companies may be significant, including understanding, implementing, and managing any technology and information systems that may be necessary.

Information Systems

Social media information systems may include the amalgam of hardware and software solutions that present an application to the end-user or customer, as Aichner et al. (2021) found, which can be utilized to perform a product lookup or search and then a follow-on monetary transaction with the company. Additionally, this monetary transaction can be the process of ordering products, reserving a seat at a restaurant, or emailing the business owner to inquire about the availability of a service. A monetary transaction may also include shipping and delivery processes that ease the burden of customer pickup at the store, a method that most consumers may wish to avoid, such as food delivery.

The information system is crucial in implementing social media technology for the business owner (van Dinter et al., 2021). Questions concerning which platforms most business customers use, and which are most straightforward to implement and maintain. A review of options should be examined concerning the costs of those implementations and how the business keeps content on these platforms fresh and interesting to its customers. Every business owner should review these questions before making strategic decisions for the company.

The strategic information systems paradigm is changing for small businesses, with several options for implementing a social media presence. The systems and options encompass various tools and platforms designed to streamline content creation, scheduling, metrics, and customer feedback (Al-Qaysi et al., 2020). The small business owner can outsource significant portions of the application rollout process while retaining control over the design process, reducing the implementation costs. However, there are information systems security concerns for any business with an online presence.

Online social media systems provide tremendous potential benefits, however, security and privacy concerns, as Ayaburi and Treku (2020) found, are also significant from a business and consumer perspective. Small businesses may lack the resources to implement robust cybersecurity measures, making them vulnerable to data breaches, unauthorized access, and other cyber threats. The sensitive and personal customer information and proprietary data handled within these systems underscore the importance of implementing stringent security protocols. Many of these security concerns can be addressed using commercial providers that can build and maintain all the operating, security, and maintenance for the information systems while leaving the updating of content and messages up to the business owner. This approach was widely implemented by many businesses.

As social media has become a significant part of small businesses' marketing strategies, as Dwivedi et al. (2021, 2023) found, it was crucial for small business owners to strike a balance between leveraging information systems for growth and safeguarding their customers and businesses' digital assets against potential security risks. Secure platforms and transactions should be built into every social media application.

Social Media Marketing

Social media marketing includes presenting ideas and capabilities to customers via social media information systems that entice the consumer to purchase a product or schedule a service (Dolega et al., 2021). Social media marketing can also be informational, as in public service announcements that provide resource availability messages to the public to bring awareness on specific issues, for example, or upcoming sales enticing customers to purchase during that sale or when a popular product was back in stock.

As Zhou (2023) indicated, companies have increasingly used social media marketing to communicate with potential consumers to influence purchasing behaviors. There was a positive link between consumer social media communication and product purchasing experiences. The link included social media marketing and online repurchasing intentions, implying a clear path for merchants to implement social media as a marketing tool to expand the consumer base and loyalty and potentially increase revenues. The idea highlighted that small businesses helped to keep social media marketing unique, relevant, and personal to build and manage repeat customer business without saturating potential customer data feeds.

The sheer breadth, reach, and impact that social media marketing has had on global consumers is staggering. As Sarin and Sharma (2023) found, specifically within the fashion industry in India, social media marketing significantly affects brand consciousness and trust, which in turn affects purchase intention and consumer loyalty.

The acceptance of social media as a marketing tool is globally understood. Still, even the American small local business owner could receive the financial benefits of implementing a social media marketing plan to capture and retain consumers, which was critical to remaining competitive.

The so-called big box stores such as Walmart, Target, and high discount stores of Costco and Sam's Club provide low-cost, cheaply made, imported products that continue to capture consumers' attention (Volpe & Boland, 2022). Those consumers are, for the most part, looking for ways to save spending resources. The small business owner needs to use social media to inform consumers about why they should visit and purchase products from their establishment. There may be higher costs in some instances, but also higher quality.

A competitive interaction between small businesses and the larger big box stores, at first glance, seems to be rather insignificant. Depending on the products offered by the small business, being competitive becomes even more important for that small business. The impact of successful social media marketing for the small business drives that ability to be more competitive by offering local goods and services that larger stores cannot. For example, where a small bookstore offers a personal experience versus walking the isles of a big box store.

A significant amount of online social media marketing and monetary exchanges was occurring, as Panda and Mishra (2023) found, where more than 65% of consumers use social media for customer service. This presents a tremendous opportunity for small businesses to tap into this market. There was significant growth in social media monetary exchanges, as indicated by Nyagadza (2020), specifically around purchasing and shipping of products utilizing third party funding applications, such as PayPal, Venmo, Google and Apple pay. These applications facilitate easy online purchases of social media driven products offered by Amazon and EBay type sources.

As van Dinter et al. (2021) indicated, the literature review delivers a more transparent, coherent, and systematic review that examines the existing knowledge and literature related to the study topic. The review process in some cases has been automated. The purpose was to utilize peer-reviewed literature that provided a meaningful and relevant guide to investigating this specific research problem. The process included selecting literature based on keywords, including social media and small business, small online businesses, online shopping, e-commerce, online retail, marketing strategies, and trends. The results were organized into a reference list that included scholarly literature, as stated before, by searching Google, Google Scholar, the University of Phoenix library, and general web-based searches.

The sample subjects of the case study were furthermore distinguished by the size of small businesses, as Alam (2021) found with those less than five hundred employees and yearly revenues of less than $5M located within the DELMARVA region. These companies were actively using social media as a marketing strategy. The Office of Advocacy for the State of Maryland, U.S. Census Bureau, provides the list of business categories and the number of employees in each business as identified by the state of Maryland. Most small businesses in the retail category have 1-19 employees, which was representative of the sample population focused in the study research.

Marketing Approach

With the advent of social media and e-commerce, a drastic change abounds where businesses and consumers are interconnected globally, eliminating the need for direct physical interaction (Wibowo et al., 2020). Online shopping continues to grow as customers' trust in e-commerce is increasing. In contrast, many commercial businesses that continue to sell in traditional brick-and-mortar stores could potentially disappear from the marketplace (Dolega et al., 2021). The value a social media presence might bring to a small company struggling to remain competitive may mean the difference between success and failure.

Within this research, the exploration of social media presence and, as Krishen et al. (2021) indicated, the implementation of social media marketing for small businesses extends beyond mere tactical implementation and examination of the data but also provides a vision of strategic innovation and ethical engagement. Through this scholarly lens, small businesses glean valuable insights into methodologies, deploying and navigating the challenging areas of digital interaction.

Social media deployment and marketing has the significant advantage of providing access to goods and services, as Dwivedi (2023) indicated, to consumers in a fast and convenient way through digital application applications. These applications provide at the consumers' fingertips, the ability to purchase just about anything that could be available through any brick-and-mortar store, as Olson et al. (2021) indicated and are normally user-friendly to use. There is the disadvantage of not being able to touch and physically see the products directly, but typically, the return process for is simple for most products. For brick-and-mortar purchases, an example might be the purchase of clothing, where the consumer wishes to try on versus, buy unseen.

Business Adaption

According to the most recent U.S. Census Bureau's (2024) release of Annual Retail Trade Survey data, e-commerce sales increased by $244.2 billion or 43% in 2020, the first year of the pandemic, rising from $571.2

billion in 2019 to $815.4 billion in 2020. According to the Small Business Administration Office of Advocacy, (2022), there were approximately 634,622 small businesses in Maryland with 1.2 million employees, accounting for 49.4% of the private workforce as seen in figures 2, 3 and 4, indicating the numbers of small businesses located in the Delaware, Maryland and Virginia areas. To provide context, these figures highlight an overall breakout and location and the numbers of small businesses in each state.

Figure 2

Small Business Profile for the State of Maryland

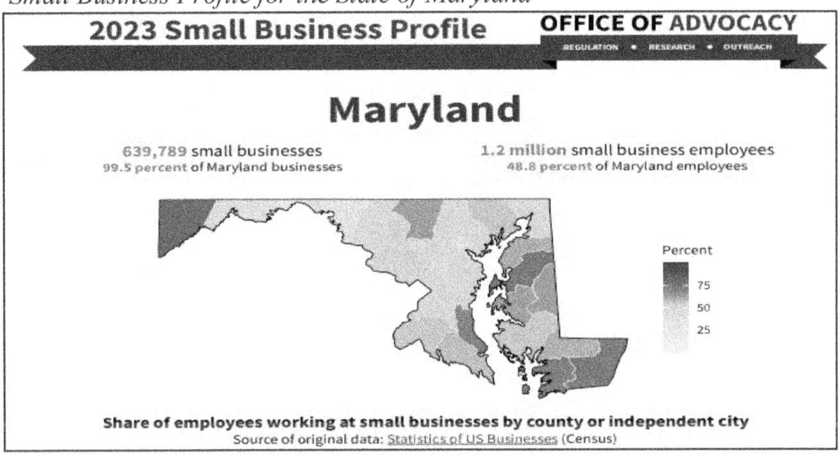

Note. Figure 2 describes the latest federal small business economics and dynamics data state by state. https://advocacy.sba.gov/2023/11/14/2023-small-business-profiles-for-thestates-territories-and-nation/.

Figure 3

Small Business Profile for the State of Delaware

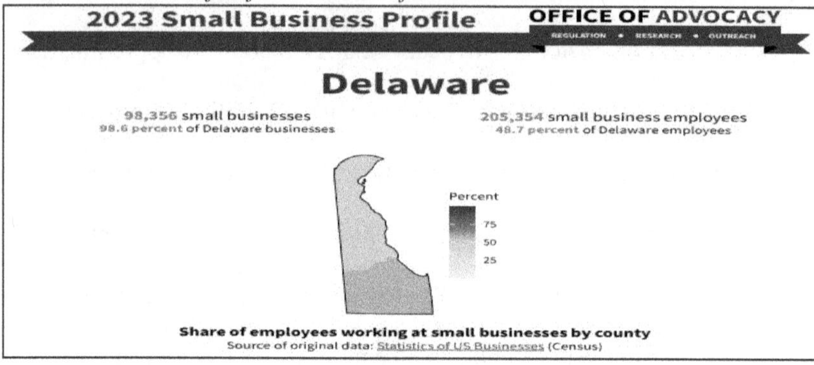

Note. Figure 3 describes the latest federal small business economics and dynamics data state by state. https://advocacy.sba.gov/2023/11/14/2023-small-business-profiles-for-thestates-territories-and-nation/.

Figure 4

Small Business Profile for the State of Virginia

Note. Figure 4 describes the latest federal small business economics and dynamics data state by state. https://advocacy.sba.gov/2023/11/14/2023-small-business-profiles-for-thestates-territories-and-nation/.

Retail revenues are expected to grow to $4.48 trillion in 2021 (Clement, 2020). The potential for revenue growth for the small business community was apparent; however, engaging consumers was the key to that success. Where the small business owner can present goods and services and engage those consumers fits into the social media marketing model well. Social media platforms facilitate scalable advertising through cost-effective and customizable campaigns. For small businesses with limited marketing budgets, this democratization of advertising allows for competitive positioning against larger firms. Paid promotions, influencer partnerships, and algorithmically targeted content amplify brand reach and can lead to exponential audience growth when executed strategically. Viewing literature and past performance techniques provided insight into that success.

Therefore, as Lin et al. (2020) indicated, this research significance includes the original contributions to topic literature, specifically to the Baltimore region area, as there are compelling gaps in research material specific to this region. Small business entrepreneurs looking to create higher revenues and bring more consumers into their venues may use social media to accomplish this goal. The value creation process should be part of every business owner's plan to build upon a company's growth (Olson et al., 2021). Viewing social media as a method to attract and retain the transient consumer population specifically within the Baltimore Metro region should provide insight into a successful roadmap from which to emulate. The adoption and implementation of social media by small businesses provided insight and clues into the ever-changing world of consumers, as indicated by Dwivedi et al. (2021), where providing in-demand items promptly in the marketplace ensures future consumer interaction and builds brand loyalty. This competitive advantage was critical to any business's success.

As Medici (2024) indicated in his article concerning marshmallow makers, small business owners in the DELMARVA region are embracing the power of social media to adapt and thrive in today's digital landscape. Recognizing the immense potential of platforms like Instagram, Facebook, and Twitter, local entrepreneurs leverage these tools to engage with their community, attract new customers, and enhance brand visibility. By fostering direct communication avenues with their target consumer base, these enterprises stay relevant and build meaningful relationships with their clientele. The target subject, small businesses in the DELMARVA region, can provide rich information about services in which these companies engage their target audience to build a loyal customer base.

This shift towards digital marketing supports small businesses' goals and objectives to reach a broader consumer audience beyond their immediate vicinity, and migrates them into a more competitive position (Lupo & Stroman, 2020). Competing with big box stores is daunting, and the lower pricing models those stores offer create issues for small establishments. Through astute analysis and strategic implementation, small businesses can navigate the intricate algorithms and evolving social media trends, creating compelling customer narratives, and cultivating interactive dialogues with consumers, like businesses found in Montana, for example (Motoyama & Henderson, 2022). Challenges occur when attracting consumers' attention with limited time and financial resources available. Small businesses are distinctly at a competitive disadvantage when offering goods and services to consumers.

Conceptual Framework Literature

The conceptual framework serves as the foundational structure upon which scholarly inquiry was constructed, offering a coherent system of concepts, assumptions, expectations, beliefs, and theories that support and inform the research endeavor. In the context of academic literature, the conceptual framework provides, as Kraus et al. (2021) describes, the researcher must have a good understanding of literature. It acts as both a lens for interpreting findings and a scaffold for designing methodology, ensuring methodological rigor and theoretical coherence.

Porter's Theory of Competitive Advantage and Shakeel Business Model Innovation

The conceptual framework is based on a model as Shakeel et al. (2020) indicated in the Business Model Innovation (BMI) in concert with Porter's (1985) theory of competitive advantage, proposed by Porter in 1985, stating that if a business holds a competitive advantage compared to rivals, this leads to a competitive advantage. Porter's four competitive benefits include and focus on cost leadership, differentiation strategy, cost-focused strategy, and differentiation-focused strategy, which was an older but truly relevant model.

Social media is a prime example of differentiation and differentiation-focused strategies (Olson et al., 2021). Cost leadership and focus depend on the small business owner's product and service pricing and providing products and services via consumerfriendly and intuitive methods. The specific type of social media technology implemented defines the competitive advantage of social media for small businesses. Understanding how a small business uses social media must first be understood.

Social Media Defined

The definition of social media is essential, as its application spans several different areas of interest, such as political, relational, and economic. Social media ecosystems are a collection of online platforms and digital communication channels designed to facilitate user creation, sharing, and exchanging of information, ideas, and multimedia content. These platforms enable individuals and organizations to connect, interact, and engage with a global audience in real-time. Social media encompasses a diverse range of platforms, as Aichner et al. (2021) found, including, but not limited to, social networking sites like Facebook, Twitter, and LinkedIn, image-sharing platforms like Instagram and Pinterest, and video-sharing platforms like YouTube.

The essence of social media lies in fostering virtual communities, enabling users to share firsthand experiences, opinions, and content, as explained by Quansah and Hartz
(2021), while also serving as a powerful tool for small business communication, marketing, and information dissemination. This, as Manzoor et al. (2020) indicated, has been the focus of the small business owner. The explosion of social media may not only affect the success of a small business, as indicated by Wang et al. (2020), but also foretell its doom to the business owner was unaware of negative social media posts or remarks concerning a

product or service. This lack of attention can spiral out of control quickly or go viral, damaging the business's reputation.

For small businesses, social media represents a dynamic and cost-effective digital medium facilitating interaction, engagement, and promotion within a targeted consumer audience. It includes online platforms, as Nyagadza (2020) found, in predictive marketing, the channels businesses can use to establish their presence, connect with new customers, and build relationships with existing ones, as Olson et al (2021) indicated microenterprise businesses utilize social media to share updates, promote products or services, and create a unique brand identity. Social media applications provide a method and a means for customer feedback, allowing businesses to respond in near or real-time, address concerns, and cultivate a sense of community around their brand. Social media for small businesses could be a significant method for building customer loyalty, gaining market insights, and adapting to the evolving preferences of their audience in a digitally interconnected world.

Several factors affect small businesses, such as hashtag-engaged consumers, as

Omena et al. (2020) indicated, and their attitudes toward purchasing products. Porter (1985) found four competitive benefits and focuses on cost leadership, differentiation strategy, cost-focused strategy, and differentiation-focused strategy, as stated before. The search into four areas of literature, cost leadership, differentiation strategy, cost-focused strategy, and differentiation-focused strategy, included more recent applications for these strategies, but for reference, Porter's model of the competitive advantage of nations is presented for review.

As Al-Qaysi et al. (2020) illustrated, the technology acceptance model illustrates forces' positive and adverse effects on a business based on competitive advantages, chance, structure, conditions, and industry type. The model identifies four vital interrelated and connected factors that influence a country, and by extension, businesses, competitiveness: factor conditions, demand conditions, related and supporting industries, firm strategy, structure, and rivalry. Factor conditions refer to a nation's resources, including human, natural, and capital resources, which influence the ability of industries to compete. Demand conditions emphasize the role of the domestic market in driving innovation and improvement. Related and small businesses and supporting industries highlight the importance of a developed and interconnected network of supporting industries. These are company strategy, structure, and rivalry, which refer to how companies are organized and compete, and are all influenced by local conditions, such as the number of small businesses in the geographic area.

Small microenterprise businesses are also influenced by how they interact with consumers. The connections of these factors create a diamond-shaped framework, illustrating how a combination of internal and external elements shape competitiveness. In the context of small businesses, the competitive advantage model serves as a framework for understanding the factors that contribute to competitiveness within their specific geographic area, which, in the research, was the DELMARVA region.

Competitive business techniques such as using social media can provide the forward momentum that small businesses need to survive and thrive, especially given the impact of large box store companies on consumer choices (Abdulwase et al., 2020). Porter's (1985) competitive advantage model describes the framework that analyzes businesses' competitive advantage. This model can also apply to the small business community as it relates to the competitive advantage that one nation has over another, much like how one small business can hold a competitive advantage over others.

Cost Leadership

An essential aspect of the contemporary business world was attributed to a competitive advantage, partly due to the growth of information technology use and the development of an internet presence (Shehata & Montash, 2020). Therefore, achieving a competitive advantage was positioning the business against its rivals to obtain greater profits and growth while creating customer value, as Gellweiler and Krishnamurthi (2020) indicated. This technology provides a process for consumers to engage with small business owners to purchase products and services and for small business owners to capitalize on the efficient marketing effects of social media.

Cost leadership through using and implementing social media has become a strategic imperative for small businesses aiming to maximize efficiency and minimize expenses. As Dwivedi et al. (2021) indicated, small businesses could reach a broad audience without incurring significant advertising costs by leveraging the power of various social media platforms.

Platforms like Facebook, Instagram, and Twitter offer cost-effective marketing tools, enabling businesses to create targeted campaigns for a specific audience of customers. Additionally, social media provides a method for customer engagement and feedback, which, in turn, fosters brand loyalty with minimal investments as compared to traditional, more random marketing methods such as print and cable media. Small businesses can implement social media's reach and engagement capabilities to build brand awareness and customer relationships at a fraction of the cost of traditional marketing methods. By strategically embracing cost leadership through social media, small businesses can compete effectively and enhance their profitability in today's highly competitive business landscape.

Differentiation Strategy

By all accounts, as Kahupi et al. (2021) found, social media was generally accepted as a competitive advantage leveraging informational delivery to potential customers on goods and services that traditional marketing methods cannot match. According to Ascend2's (2018) list of strategic priorities to create a differentiation strategy, includes increasing sales, acquisition, customer engagement, brand awareness, result measurement or Key Performance Indicators (KPI), website traffic, and web user experience. If adopted by the small business owner, using these strategies can potentially differentiate businesses from others in the marketplace. Customer engagement and brand awareness seem excellent starting points for web and social media experiences, where the business owner encourages in-store consumers to visit their social media page or website.

Business strategies can be understood as growth imperatives as Banerjee et al. (2020) indicated, where this imperative provides a financial foundation for all organizational activities, generates employment, drives improvements in living standards, provides benefits to individuals and communities through wealth creation, and can result in greater consumer choice. Economic growth offers a set of widely shared goals that galvanize organizational purpose and provide readily measurable outcomes to guide business strategies.

Olson et al. (2021) indicated that considering specific digital marketing tactics, content marketing and search engine optimization are one of the most valued customer captured processes. In a differentiation strategy, a business endeavors to be unique and provide goods and services along the business's product lines, presenting significant consumer value and describing how the small business owner can create this differentiation by implementing social media to enhance brand awareness and ease the purchase process, thereby improving sales.

The small business owner aims to remain competitive, grow brand identity, and build customer loyalty (Olson et al., 2021). Differentiating small businesses from similar small businesses in the same local area required unique ways to connect with and retain customers. To discover how the subject small business owners accomplished this, the interview process provided some insight and vision that each business owner had when working towards implementing a social media presence.

Cost Focused Strategy

As Abdulwase et al. (2020) indicated, a cost-focused strategy concerns how the business offers and focuses on cost control and securing a more extensive consumer base by offering lower overall costs to their customers. Low-cost businesses typically provide few, if any, ancillary services and tend to operate in well-established and stable markets. Some examples include Walmart, Costco, Target, and Aldi, to name a few. In striving for a cost advantage over rivals, small business owners must incorporate features and services that buyers consider essential; these features can be expressed through social media.

A cost-focused strategy for small businesses utilizing social media involves a deliberate and efficient allocation of resources to maximize the impact of online presence while minimizing expenses and costs (Abdulwase et al., 2020). Small businesses, often operating with limited budgets, can leverage social media platforms strategically to achieve their goals without significant financial strain. By utilizing free or low-cost analytics tools, the small business owner can measure the effectiveness of their social media efforts and refine their strategies accordingly. By adopting a cost-focused strategy in social media utilization, small businesses can enhance their online presence, engage with their target audience effectively, and achieve their business objectives without consuming precious resources.

Differentiation-Focused Strategy

By all accounts, competitive advantage stems from a company's strategic choices to seize market opportunities. The competitive advantage inherent to a company's performance was its ability to distinguish itself from competitors through interaction in providing products, goods, or services. A differentiation-focused strategy can include the competitive strategy, as Olson et al. (2021) found, used by small businesses where companies build and develop various strategic resources with the potential to generate competitive advantage, such as innovative social media marketing tools. The competitive advantage can be achieved if customers observe and understand a consistent and persistent difference within a small business's marketing, offerings, and engagements.

This perception can then attain growth through word of mouth between consumers and perpetuate customer loyalty, one of the main goals of any small business.

Small businesses adopting a differentiation-focused strategy in their use of social media need to leverage their unique and distinctive elements to set themselves apart in the digital landscape (Olson et al., 2021). These businesses should focus on creating a memorable and remarkable online presence through creative content, personalized engagement, and strategic branding efforts on platforms like Facebook, Instagram, and Twitter. Differentiating one small business with the same general business model, offering the same general product lines, from any other business should include marketing and customer engagement in ways other companies may not. Targeted emails with new product offerings, updated web displays, and text-to-phone messages may differentiate one business from another. Care must be taken to keep small business consumers from unwanted ads and needless verbiage.

The small business owner should happily receive and encourage consumer feedback, as Quansah and Hartz (2021) found, to adjust and control the right amount of interaction concerning social media and marketing processes. This feedback from consumers and the resulting control of social media interaction was a significant differentiator between businesses and could mean the difference between retaining and losing customers. This interaction between business owners and consumers provides a strategic advantage that differentiates some stores from others. This interaction offers the consumer a sense of understanding and appreciation in that the business owner cares qualitatively about the consumer's interests and concerns. This interaction can be in person or via message services built into the social media presence, but the interaction could be the differentiator consumers use to make future purchasing decisions. The "I like this store because they take care of me and understand and fix problems when they occur" feedback was excellent marketing material for small businesses and builds brand awareness and consumer loyalty.

Qualitative study in this domain explores how small businesses strategically differentiate themselves in a crowded market through social media, emphasizing innovative content creation, customer experience, and building and cultivating a unique brand identity (Sarin & Sharma, 2023). The literature suggests that such an approach allows small enterprises to carve out a niche, foster customer loyalty, and effectively compete in the dynamic digital marketplace while focusing on delivering unique value to their target audience.

Methodology Literature

Qualitative methodology plays a pivotal role in social sciences and humanities, offering a nuanced and in-depth exploration of human experiences, perspectives, and behaviors (Emiliussen et al., 2021). Qualitative methodologies focus on interviews, observations, and content analysis; qualitative research seeks to uncover the richness and complexity of the social world. These methods of data collection prioritize content, allowing researchers to delve into the intricacies of individual narratives and societal phenomena. Qualitative methodology provides a holistic understanding of the subjective aspects of human existence, allowing researchers to explore not just "what" but also "why" and "how." Through its emphasis on interpretive analysis, qualitative methodology contributes significantly to our comprehension of cultural, social, and psychological phenomena, providing a deeper and more contextually grounded insight into the intricacies of the human condition.

Qualitative methodology must incorporate rigorous data collection suitable interview protocols for collection and analysis, multiple steps in data analysis, and characteristics that have ensured the quality of the research (Liamputtong, 2020). A qualitative research study should include an abstract section summarizing the report, including background information, research questions, methods, and results (Creswell & Báez, 2020). In addition, it was essential to explain the qualitative research design used for the study, such as grounded theory, ethnography, narrative inquiry, case study, and phenomenology, as well as the sample size appropriate for the study (Paparini et al., 2020).

Analytic generalization was part of this study qualitative research methodology, as Maxwell (2021) indicated. According to Maxwell (2021), data generalization has been divided into two types: statistical generalization, associated with quantitative research, and analytic generalization, used with qualitative research (Maxwell, 2021). Information captured during this study fell into analytic generalization using coding techniques to categorize the data.

Qualitative Methods and Business-Based Research

The qualitative research method interacts well with business-based subject matter that requires interactive and reflective reviews involving participant perspectives, specifically for business owners, as Singh et al. (2021) indicated, and was also inductive and unstructured where the explanation for the experience of how a business owner may have come to the reasoning for implementing social media may elude the interviewer. The reasoning behind the small business owner's implementation of social media should be understood as an indicator for entrepreneurs looking for means to explore and complement current marketing techniques. The rational for implementing social media in the small business environment can shed interesting light for other business owners, entertaining the reasoning of social media, the effort required to build and maintain a social media presence, and the potential benefits. There are also consumer considerations to examine.

These qualitative case studies provided interesting viewpoints on the qualitative case study approach process. Potentially interesting perspectives and viewpoints are that small businesses can use social media to create competitive advantages rivaling large ones. Social media can sway any business in both a positive and negative way. Social media has also only become more prevalent in the few years as a business-marketing tool and will continue to grow in the future.

Several studies related to social media such as marketing, branding, and business engagement tools have been completed. Park et al. (2020) found the branding power where small business owners that are responsible for their own social media branding much like Division 1 university students, where eleven student-athletes could run afoul of appropriate social media branding. These athletes participated in semi-structured interviews and have shed awareness on the use and potential negative consequences of using social media branding for university students. Negative feedback from social media created issues for these students found, in the Park et al. (2020) study, as it could for any business that needs a clear plan for goals and objectives for social media implementation.

Obermayer et al. (2022) found how social media shaped perceptions of family wineries located in the Balaton region of Hungary. Using the case study method, six wineries were selected from a pool of fifty-five to participate in semi-structured interviews. Obermayer et al.'s goal for the study was to understand the marketing tools implemented to improve customer awareness and brand recognition (Obermayer et al., 2022). The importance of Obermayer et al.'s 2022 study was that branding and consumer loyalty are built upon companies' marketing techniques, where social media can be influential.

Fatima and Ali (2023) found that businesspersons running a small enterprise in Spain used social media to engage customers. The researchers found that family and friends were influential in the social media decisions these businesspersons made. Even though they were women owned small businesses, their family groups understood the influence social media could have. The study also found that combining traditional and social media could improve customer engagement. Consumers and business owners alike understand the importance of social media as a critical factor in interpersonal activity.

The steps a researcher must take to develop a qualitative case study include identifying and defining the problem and selecting research subjects (Khalifa et al., 2020). When describing the problem, attention was given to research questions, defining the study framework, and building research alignment throughout each study to address the research question. Developing a qualitative research study involves a systematic and thoughtful process to explore and understand the depth and nuances of a particular phenomenon.

The research aims to review existing literature to understand the current knowledge in the chosen field. Following this, selecting an appropriate research design, such as a case study, ethnography, or grounded theory, was crucial. The study should carefully consider the sampling technique to select an appropriate, diverse, representative participant group. Data collection methods, such as interviews, online surveys, and observations, were chosen based on potential research questions and design. Rigorous data analysis involving coding, categorization, and interpretation was then undertaken to derive meaningful insights. Ethical considerations, such as participant confidentiality and informed consent, observation techniques, and obscuring owner and customer private information has been critical throughout the research.

As Dwivedi et al. (2023) found, a number of consumer interactions need to be considered when they involve exchanging funds in online monetary transactions. The security considerations expand when user information is captured through online cookies and other personal information, as well as the data retention related to any consumer information. A straightforward, understandable method of consumer interactions should be reviewed before customer interaction, especially if the small business owner offers online personal or monetary interactions.

The monetary interaction between consumers and small business owners can be explored during the qualitative interview between the researcher and the small business owner (Dwivedi et al., 2021). Additionally, some of the challenges encountered during the development of online transactions can be analyzed and teased out to better understand that part of the implementation process. Security has been a significant concern when business owners implement a monetary transaction system, and many small businesses have encountered this internet challenge in the past, as several studies on the use of social media have been published.

Qualitative Study Related to Small Business Use of Social Media

There are many other qualitative studies related to the topic of social media. For example, a study was conducted in 2018 to research the effective Internet marketing strategies of small online fashion jewelry businesses. These multiple case study interviewed three business owners who owned online fashion jewelry businesses in the northeastern U.S. The findings of this study resulted in six key themes, including e-mail, the internet, the social media market space, brand building, market research, and retargeting strategies (Daemi et al., 2021).

Researchers adopting qualitative methodologies delve into small business owners nuanced experiences, perceptions, and decision-making processes as they navigate the dynamic realm of social media marketing; the study by Obermayer et al. (2022) found that wineries in Hungary served as an example of this process. Qualitative research typically employs in-depth interviews, focus groups, content analysis, and participant observation to capture the richness of participants' narratives and the subtleties of their interactions on social media platforms.

Through exploring users lived experiences, the qualitative approach contributes valuable insights that complement quantitative data, offering a more holistic understanding of the complex dynamics surrounding social media in contemporary society. Researchers adopting a qualitative approach emphasize the importance of context, allowing for a deeper exploration of the social, cultural, and psychological dimensions that influence individuals' engagement with and perceptions of social media.

Research Design Literature

A qualitative exploratory multiple case study, as Schoch (2020) found, delves into the intricacies of the phenomenon within the study, allowing research into the various perspectives, perceptions feelings, and contexts influencing the phenomenon. The approach to case study includes understanding the experiences, perceptions, behaviors, and as Stake (1995) indicates a strong motivation for discovering meaning understanding experiences in context. The study also seeks to identify patterns, themes, or relationships that emerge from the data, as Stake and Visse (2022) indicates the how and why to develop a comprehensive understanding of the phenomenon.

Qualitative Case Study

The chosen research design was a case study; as Farquhar et al. (2020) indicated, a case study involves in-depth research into one or a small set of cases. The goal of a case study was to capture a detailed understanding of a particular subject and was viewed as the blueprint for the research. This qualitative exploratory multiple case study was focused, as Merriam (1998) on a particular thing, that is in part the acceptance and usage of social media as a replacement technology for traditional marketing within the theoretical framework and was implemented to attract and retain the transient consumer base in the DELMARVA region. Although Qualitative in nature, case study is especially context-oriented (Yin, 2017).

Some concepts surrounding social media implementation included value, company loyalty, financial benefits, and technology deployment, underpinning small businesses' challenges in transitioning from traditional to social media marketing. As

Shultz et al. (2020) indicated, as an overall approach, case study research is based on indepth explorations of complex phenomena in their natural or real-life settings. As Creswell and Báez (2020) indicated, case study researchers develop an in-depth analysis of an activity or process bounded by time.

Moghadam et al. (2021) indicated that case study research contains five stages:

defining the research question, instrument development and site selection, data gathering, analysis, and dissemination of the investigation. The Moghadam et al. (2021) case study model contains the five elements supporting the understanding of the transition from traditional to social media marketing technology use, which underlines the contextual confusion between the two technologies and the challenges involved.

The case study model and design align and are appropriate within the definition of a case study in capturing business owner experiences through research questions (Farquhar et al., 2020). The model also addresses the lived challenges and experiences, connecting and aligning the purpose of this qualitative exploratory multiple case study with documenting the issues and trends, all within the conceptual framework for this study. The qualitative exploratory multiple case study methodology was deemed highly appropriate in various research contexts, mainly when an in-depth understanding of a phenomenon within its real-life context was essential.

Qualitative case study allows for a detailed examination of a specific case or case, often-employing interviews, observations, and document analysis. Qualitative methodology was well suited for research questions that require an exploration of the intricacies, processes, and social dynamics surrounding a particular phenomenon. The appropriateness of qualitative case study was particularly evident when researchers aim to generate rich, detailed insights and when the focus was on understanding the depth and complexity of a specific situation or phenomenon rather than generalizing findings to a larger population.

The exploratory case study research on small businesses leveraging social media presents a compelling investigation into the dynamic landscape of contemporary entrepreneurship (Shultz et al., 2020). By examining a variety of small businesses across industries, case study research may be used to identify common trends, challenges, and success stories or areas where social media did not work for business owners. Based on reviewing Shultz et al. (2020), a goal for this exploratory multiple case study was to shed light on the innovative ways small businesses utilize social media and contribute insights to the evolving role of digital platforms in the modern business landscape.

A multiple case study provides for broader and richer content coverage, where several different perspectives are captured and coalesced into a deeper understanding of a phenomenon. A multiple case study, as indicated by Halkias et al. (2023) is a valuable research tool in studying connections between internal organizational environments and personal perspectives on phenomenon within a business community. The Halkias et al. (2023) reference includes how a case study aligns with a research goal that was met by answering phenomenon-based questions such as how or why something happens. Case study, as indicated by Halkias et al. (2023) are performed for several reasons and are appropriate when the researcher has an interest in the subject or desires an in-depth understanding of a phenomenon.

In performing the literature review research and investigation of social media use by family-owned microenterprises, the strategies employed by small businesses as microenterprises navigate the expansive realm of social media platforms was reviewed and examined. Through a qualitative lens, this research attempts to understand the diverse approaches that small businesses adopted to harness the power of online networks and electronic media for marketing, customer engagement, and brand building. The literature reviewed research focused on understanding the diverse approaches that small businesses adopted to harness the power of online networks for marketing, customer engagement, and brand building.

In reviewing the literature available on small business use of social media, multiple articles underscore the transformative role in contemporary commerce (Dwivedi et al., 2021, 2023). Numerous studies, such as Li et al.,

(2021) Naslund et al., (2021) or Cartwright et al., (2021), explored the strategies, challenges, and outcomes of integrating social media platforms into small business operations. Scholars such as Li et al., Naslund et al., and Cartwright et al., have explored how small enterprises leverage platforms like Facebook, Instagram, and Twitter for marketing, brand building, and customer engagement.

Research found in the literature review emphasized the importance of understanding the unique dynamics that influence small businesses' adoption and management of social media strategies, such as resource constraints by Fu and Timothy (2021), creative content development by Marsiana et al. (2022), and community building by Glazier and Topping (2021). The literature consistently underscored the significance of social media in providing cost-effective avenues for visibility, customer interaction, and competitive positioning for small businesses in a crowded marketplace by providing insight on potential resources, content development and community issues that could arise.

Moreover, researchers such as Fu and Timothy (2021), Marsiana et al., (2022), and Glazier and Topping (2021), recognized the need for a nuanced understanding of the social, cultural, and psychological dimensions that shape small business owner perceptions and decision-making processes using social media platforms. The social, cultural, and psychological dimensions included why a small business owner would likely invest the time, resources, and effort into implementing a social media presence and deploying the technology.

The literature review conducted for this research provided a comprehensive examination of social media's multifaceted role, as indicated by Kaye (2021) in transforming a knowledge society (Aichner et al., 2021). The exploration encompassed various dimensions, including the role of social media on information dissemination, knowledge sharing, as indicated by Alalwan et al. (2016), in collaborative learning on small business subjects. Attention was also given to the challenges associated with the increased reliance on social media, such as information credibility, the digital divide, and the ethical implications of data sharing between small businesses and consumers of products from those businesses.

Conclusions

Several conclusions emerged through conducting the literature review, (Aichner et al., 2021). Social media has created an explosion of information available at the consumer's fingertips, and the small business owner can capture and build on company success (Dwivedi et al., 2023). The tectonic shift in business methods has significantly influenced small businesses, their branding power, and their ability to attract consumers.

The literature review showed limited information and data available in historical and current research specific to the DELMARVA region was available.

Some additional conclusions based on the literature review were as follows. First, the growth of e-commerce has revolutionized the business world throughout the years and was now reshaping its future (Briar-Lawson et al., 2020). Second, the exponential global rise of social media and e-commerce in recent years created online business opportunities and challenges for small businesses, including the need to stay competitive and profitable, as Sajjad and Zaman (2020) indicated. Third, a clear understanding of the complexities and resources the business owner must invest in this technology, both in monetary and human resources, should be part of a value-added proposition. The microenterprise owner must understand that the business commitment to social media was iterative, potentially resource-intensive, and requires close attention to detail concerning customer interactions.

As Zhang et al. (2023) also found, the literature underscored social media's transformative nature in reshaping the literature landscape concerning social media technologies, offering opportunities and challenges. The current literature review's goal was to engage critically with social media literature, to recognize the power to shape cultural narratives while being mindful of the responsibilities that comes with social media as a technology. Additional goals included attending to literary gaps and contributing to academia while examining how small businesses attract and compete for transient consumers in the DELMARVA region.

Chapter Summary

Chapter 2 began with a description of the purpose of this exploratory multiple case study and an explanation of the processes followed in conducting the literature review (Schoch, 2020). Several keywords, such as business owners, small online businesses, online shopping, e-commerce, online retail, marketing strategies, and trends, were included in a plan to search to locate the literature available. While the literature included some historical and current literature in journals and articles, specifically with regard to research papers related to the topic of the small business owner in the DELMARVA region attracting consumers, there needed to be more information that is relevant. There was, however, extensive literature on social media as a general subject related to business.

There was a preponderance of literature on social media due to the expansive growth in the use and acceptance of technology (Aichner et al., 2021). The topic of social media is vast and the focus on one area of research often leads the researcher into different, frequently unrelated regions of the topic. To solve this dilemma in part, the focus on the primary subject matter of the small microenterprise business owners in the DELMARVA region must always be maintained to solve this dilemma in part. Researching the specific subject matter of small businesses narrows the literature search, and adding particular keywords focusing on the DELMARVA region, specifically the Baltimore area as the target community added even tighter research parameters.

The literature review was critical to examine the research of the subject matter, social media and small business use in the DELMARVA region, and what data or information was available to draw qualitative opinions and ideas (Aichner et al., 2021).

The gap in available information provided a venue to lend innovative ideas to academia, latest ideas for entrepreneurs, and a framework from which small business owners contemplating the implementation of social media could work. The present study attempted to bridge the research gap of why small businesses determine the need for social media technology to attract customers, including a highly transient group living in the DELMARVA region.

Chapter 1 provided an overview of the study, describing the research background, problem, and purpose. Also described were terms, assumption, limitations, and delimitations. The significance of the study and research questions were also provided in Chapter 1. Chapter 2 described the research design literature, methodologies in literature, conceptual frameworks, descriptions of research methodologies and background theories explored. Chapter 3 addresses the research methodology, method and design, the participant population, and the sample size. Also described in Chapter 3 was the consent and confidentiality process, and the ethical considerations, along with the instrumentation used. Creditability and transferability are also described along with the data collection
processes and some early analysis.

Chapter 3

Research Methodology

In Chapter 1, the purpose of this qualitative exploratory multiple case study was addressed. The purpose of the qualitative exploratory multiple case study was to examine the perceptions of owners and employees at family-owned microenterprises regarding their reasons for implementing social media strategies, the success of those strategies, and the challenges faced in using those strategies in a highly transient DELMARVA region. Chapter 2 presented the theoretical foundations of and background literature for the study, plus literature relating to certain aspects of the methodology.

Chapter 3 presents the research methodology for the research. Chapter 3 begins with the research method and design, explicating the discussion of these topics addressed in Chapter 1. Then, the research questions guiding the study are revisited. The population and sample for the study are discussed. The issues of informed consent and confidentiality are detailed. The instruments used in data collection for the research study are discussed. A discussion of the field test has been presented and followed by a discussion of credibility and transferability in this study. Following the discussion of credibility and transferability, the data collection and data analysis sections are presented.

Chapter 3 concludes with a summary of key points.

Research Method and Design Appropriateness

A qualitative research method was adopted for conducting this research.

Qualitative research was an open-ended and exploratory research method (Merriam & Tisdell, 2015). A qualitative study is typically focused on a broadly defined central research phenomenon (Liamputtong, 2020). The breadth of the phenomena studied by qualitative researchers necessitates a more open-ended approach to conducting research (Merriam & Tisdell, 2015).

Qualitative description research necessarily casts a wide net, thereby capturing significant aspects of the context surrounding the central research phenomenon in addition to that phenomenon itself (Liamputtong, 2020). Because of its open-ended nature and being well suited to studying broad phenomena, qualitative research was also ideal for exploring new ideas (Liamputtong, 2020). Additionally, the open-endedness of qualitative research necessitates a descriptive approach to research in which a researcher explores the perceptions of key population groups through open-ended description (Merriam & Tisdell, 2015).

The use of qualitative methodology aligned with this study for a series of key reasons. First, the purpose of the qualitative exploratory multiple case study was in alignment with the open-ended, broad, and contextualized nature of qualitative research. Second, the purpose of the qualitative exploratory multiple case study was to explore and discover the perceptions of owners and employees at family-owned microenterprises in the DELMARVA region regarding their reasons for implementing social media strategies. Lastly, part of the current research was to understand how the owners and employees in these microenterprises to learn more about the success of the selected social media strategies and the challenges faced in using those strategies.

As the research phenomenon was broad, given that strategies are also a broad topic, qualitative research made sense. Additionally, the success of the social media strategies used and the challenges such strategies brought were best captured descriptively. Further, the research was deeply contextual because of a focus on the specific context of family-owned microenterprises in a given region of the United States. In addition, the study was highly contextual due to its focus on a transient area in a given region of the United States.

Within qualitative methodology, there are many specific research designs that a researcher may adopt. Qualitative multiple case study made the most sense for this research as it provided deep, rich insight into the challenges and successes that the microenterprise business owner encountered during and after social media implementation. Although all qualitative research is contextual in nature, the defining feature of a case study is that it is especially context-oriented (Yin, 2017). Case study, as Farquhar et al., (2020) indicated involves in-depth into a small set of cases or subjects. The case study model, as Farquhar (2020) indicates captures the experiences through research questions.

There are several types of case study designs such as descriptive, intrinsic, instrumental, illustrative, cumulative, or critical instances. Exploratory case study was used for this research and completed using the multiple case study design. Exploratory case study designs are used when the topic is new, as is the case with family-owned microenterprises using social media, and not well understood (Stake, 2008). An exploratory case study offers a preliminary understanding of the central research phenomenon (Yin, 2017).

An exploratory multiple case study design was the best qualitative research design for this research for several vital reasons. The present research was particularly contextual on two levels. This research addresses not only the contextual dimension of family-owned microenterprises that may offer different services but also the contextual dimension of a transient DELMARVA region. Social media strategies are implemented at multiple levels, shaping the study context (Halkias et al., 2023). Therefore, a multiple case study was ideal because of the ability to use various sources of data to undertake a more thorough exploration that allows for a fuller exploration of distinct levels of social media strategy (Halkias et al., 2023).

The multiple case study design, as indicated by Halkias et al. (2023), was a valuable research tool for studying connections between business environments and leadership perspectives on phenomena within their environment. The process included how a case study aligns with a research goal that was met by answering object-based questions such as how or why something happens. Case studies also, as indicated by Halkias et al. (2023), are performed for several reasons and, more importantly, are appropriate when the researcher has a significant interest in a subject and desires an indepth understanding of a phenomenon. The multiple case study design provides a more profound and richer content coverage, subjectively capturing different perspectives that coalesce into a more significant understanding of a phenomenon.

Furthermore, by adopting an exploratory multiple case approach, it has been possible to compare different specific contexts. By applying an exploratory multiple case study design, the research study addresses a topic that was not yet well understood. The exploratory case study, as indicated by Hancock et al. (2021) provides a valuable guide for the "what" of the research and then the "why" that research was important, with a goal of a greater understanding of the phenomenon of the research. There are alternatives to exploratory case research though.

Alternative Designs Considered

Several alternative qualitative research designs were also considered. One alternate design was phenomenology. A phenomenological study involves in-depth exploration of the participants lived experiences (Moustakas, 1994). This study, however, was concerned with understanding broader strategies and enhanced relevance, not people's specific experiences. As such, the greater depth of phenomenology, or the essence of lived experience would afford little extra benefit.

Another design considered was grounded theory. Grounded theory involves developing new theory from raw data or validating an existing theory (Strauss & Corbin, 1997). This study, however, already has a conceptual framework, the BMI (Gassmann et al., 2016) and Porter's (1985) theory of competitive advantage. Both are validated concepts and theories within the business community. Therefore, the study does not require a grounded theory approach.

A third design considered was ethnography. Ethnography involves the study of the customs of an intact ethnic, cultural, or subcultural group (Hirsch & Gellner, 2020). Although this study does focus on a specific group, namely microenterprise owners and employees, this group was not ethnically, culturally, or sub-culturally defined in such a way as to make ethnography appropriate. The study focused not on the customs of an ethnic, cultural, or subcultural group but on the processes and practices connected to social media choices for micro entrepreneurial organizations. Understanding these processes and practices has been captured through research inquiry and questions used during the data capture period.

Research Questions

In the qualitative exploratory multiple case study, three goals existed. One goal was to understand the reasons why those small family-operated microenterprise business owners implemented social media marketing and employee use; another goal was to perceive the successes or failures in the marketing endeavor and how easy or hard that process was. A third goal was to understand the capabilities the technology provided owners to interact with customers. To achieve these goals, three research questions that guide the research study:

R1: What are the owner perceptions at family-owned microenterprises in the

DELMARVA region regarding their reasons for implementing social media strategies?

R2: What are the employee perceptions at family-owned microenterprises in the DELMARVA region regarding the influence with customers concerning business social media strategies?

R3: What are the customer perceptions at family-owned microenterprises in the DELMARVA region regarding accuracy and usability of the social media interfaces?

Population and Sample

The population sample focused on a specific group that a researcher was interested in understanding when conducting research (Banerjee & Chaudhury, 2010). This population criterion sample included five small, or microenterprise businesses, with five or fewer employees and limited revenues. For the research study, the overall population was microenterprise owners, employees, and customers, in a transient area within the US Mid-Atlantic states, which include Delaware, Maryland, and Virginia also colloquially referred to as the DELMARVA region. Microenterprises are the smallest category of small businesses, those with fewer than five employees (Handayani, 2023). Many microenterprises are family businesses simply because family businesses tend to be small.

Within this overall population, the target population and criteria for the participants were family-owned microenterprise owners, employees, and customers, in the transient DELMARVA region. The target population was the group from which the researcher recruited participants (Banerjee &

Chaudhury, 2010). In defining the target population, the transience of the region was expected to play a significant role in the types of social media strategies used and their efficacy. The inclusion criteria specified that all participants must (a) be at least 18 years of age, (b) own or work for a familyowned microenterprise, and (c) live and be a customer in the transient DELMARVA region of interest.

A sample represents the specific group of study participants (Banerjee & Chaudhury, 2010). Within this population, five specific microenterprises were selected as case study “see Table 5”. These five cases provided the research sample, and although limited in number, represented several diverse types of microenterprises. The final sample of five business owners “see Table 3”, five employees “see Table 4” and at least five customers from each business case was selected as excellent representation. The criterion sampling strategy was purposive in nature, where each sample followed a specific criterion, as this strategy enhances the rigor of the study (Campbell et al., 2020).

Using a criterion purposive sampling technique, participants were chosen for the relevance to answering the study research questions, as an owner, employee, or a customer of the microenterprise (Etikan et al., 2016). Participants were recruited using purposive criterion sampling, the criteria was based on small, family-owned microenterprises, having fewer than five employees and limited revenues to five million dollars. One owner from each business and an employee from each of the five businesses participated using an email containing a Microsoft Word document with questions. Additional data were gathered from customers via an online survey. For each microenterprise, the online social media application of each business, that is, Facebook, web pages, and other systems such as Nextdoor, were also perused and reviewed to capture consumer feedback on each business. All data capture was completed using human subject standards for confidentiality.

Informed Consent and Confidentiality

Ethical research practices were strictly followed when collecting data. As a preliminary step, the five businesses were selected and contacted, and sent site consent to conduct the research (see Appendix C) documents to sign. In addition, each individual participant also completed an informed consent form covering the interview as appropriate. Informed consent forms detailed the research in depth, including the expected requirements of participation. The form also provided for the inclusion criteria, the measures taken to protect participants' confidentiality, and the possible academic benefits of the study. The signed informed consent forms, were uploaded to the electronic signature service DocuSign for ease of access (see Appendix D) and controlled exposure or capture using less secure email methods.

Participants' confidentiality was carefully protected at every stage of the research. Only the researcher and approved university personnel had access to identifying information about the participants. Within the study, participants were assigned numbers or letters to protect their confidentiality. Any potentially identifying information in the study has been redacted. All data were stored securely on an encrypted flash drive when not in use. The USB flash drive plus any physical printouts were kept in a locked desk drawer. All data will be preserved for three years after completion of the study, then fully erased, shredded, destroyed or deleted as appropriate per the medium used.

Instrumentation

Interviews are a pivotal research instrument in qualitative research, providing a rich, nuanced understanding of participants' experiences and perspectives. Unlike quantitative methods that rely on numerical data, interviews allow for in-depth exploration of complex issues through open-ended questions, enabling researchers to capture the subtleties of human behavior and thought processes (Tavory, 2020).

Conducting interviews involves a systematic approach, beginning with the formulation of a clear interview guide that aligns with the research objectives. The interview guide ensures consistency while allowing flexibility for probing deeper into interesting or unexpected responses (Tavory, 2020). The interpersonal nature of interviews fosters a rapport between the interviewer and the interviewee, which can lead to more candid and detailed responses. However, this method also requires careful attention to ethical considerations, such as informed consent and confidentiality, to protect participants' rights and well-being (Kakilla, 2021). Overall, interviews are a valuable tool for gaining comprehensive insights, which might be overlooked by other research methods.

Semi-Structured Interviews

The first and primary method of data collection has been qualitative, semistructured interviews with a protocol. Semi-structured interviews are the main approach researchers use to collect qualitative data (Kallio et al., 2016). Semi-structured interviews use a protocol, or guide, to assist researchers in data collection. These interviews offer a balanced approach, both structured and flexible, while offering in-depth insight into the participants' perspectives (Ruslin et al., 2022).

Semi-structured interviews have two main components. The first component in the structure was an interview guide (see Appendix E). An interview guide is a set of preliminary questions and topics that guide the interview (Kallio et al., 2016). The focus of the interview guide was to ensure that the data collected in the interview sufficiently addresses the research questions guiding the study (Ruslin et al., 2022).

To this end, an expert panel from within the university was recruited to review and improve the interview guide. However, the other half of a semi-structured interview was the unstructured follow-up or probing questions that the researcher may ask during the interview process (Kallio et al., 2016). These questions were used as needed to clarify key points during the interviews to ensure that the data collection was appropriately comprehensive.

The questions contained in Table 2 are consistent between methods of delivery and aligned within the email instrument used.

Table 2

Alignment of Interview Questions to the Research Questions

Research Questions	Interview Questions
R1: What are the owner perceptions at familyowned microenterprises in the DELMARVA region regarding their reasons for implementing social media strategies?	1. Please describe how long your company has been doing business. 2. Please briefly describe the type of business that you own. 3. Please describe what social media applications you are using now, for example, Facebook, Yelp, or a website. 4. Please describe your social media marketing strategies to increase revenues or client exposure. 5. Please discuss the benefits you have experienced using social media. 6. Please describe any situations or unexpected issues or problems you encountered using social media. 7. Please explain the process you went through to get from initial implementation to where you are today. 8. Please describe any persistent or ongoing problems you may be experiencing using social media.
R2: What are the employee perceptions at family-owned microenterprises in the DELMARVA region regarding the influence with customers concerning business social media strategies?	1. Please explain what social media training was required for the applications used by the business. 2. Please describe how often you use social media for business purposes (e.g., using a store application to look up a product for a customer). 3. Please describe how the organization could use social media differently. 4. Please explain how customers have used social media applications to visit the store. 5. Please explain if your employer utilizes social media to its fullest. 6. Please explain how social media has made your job easier or more difficult. 7. Please explain your personal feelings about using social media as a technology and a means of communication.

R3: What are the customer perceptions of family-owned microenterprises in the DELMARVA region regarding accuracy and usability of the social media interfaces?	1. Please explain the benefits you experienced in using social media for locating businesses. 2. Please explain how social media influences purchasing decisions. 3. As a customer, what is your experience using social media to find or evaluate small businesses before engaging with them? 4. Please explain the importance of a business's social media presence to you. 5. As a customer when you decide to interact with a business, how important is the small business's social media presence in that decision? 6. Please explain how you use social media to evaluate a business. 7. Please describe a positive or negative business-related social media experience. 8. Please explain any feedback you may have provided to a business via social media.

Note. Table 2 denotes the alignment between interview questions and RQs (Wieland, 2024)

Artifact Collection

The secondary data collection sourcc of data was the inclusion of artifact collection. Artifact collection took on several forms. First, after signing permission to use interviews, the researcher located published sources of information such as local newspaper clippings, online articles concerning the business, and any printed sources of information that might be insightful. In many cases, there was not a significant amount of that information.

The second source of artifact collection included the social media presence of the businesses. Social media presence was documented through screenshots of the current social media postings and overall presence of each business including online applications. The content analysis for artifact review included a listing of favorable and unfavorable remarks and have been indicated in a point system. In situations where both attitudes are expressed, a point in each column was also added.

Excellent content and data management are often overlooked (Kanza & Knight, 2022). Data collection and content analysis for artifacts started with folder creations for each of the participants. Each folder contains copies of audio and paper transcriptions of each interview. A coded collection for each subject was also included in each folder, and all participant identities have been protected. No participant identities have been captured, rather a lettering system was utilized to identify each different business, using letters A through E.

The folders have been encrypted and password protected to prevent data breaches. All data will be stored for three years and backed up to a USB flash drive that will also be stored for three years. At the end of that period, the USB flash drive will be erased and then crushed, the existing data on the PC drive will be erased and that drive will be reformatted.

Field Test

A field test was conducted to test the instrumentation. Because recruiting additional interviewees for field-testing was not feasible, the interview discussion questions were field tested, and the results were then used to develop the employee and customer questions. The field test involved recruiting participants with expert knowledge in the area of research or one business owner plus an employee from that business. This business owner and employee met the inclusion criteria for the study, but whose business was not one of the five case studies.

The field test also included an electronic mail instrument that included the same set of questions and followed the same theme of the research questions provided in the interview process. These field tests were completed prior to seeking Institutional Review Board (IRB) approval. A field test interview was conducted to refine the interview discussion questions. The field test interview responses helped further shape the interview research protocol. The results of the field test were used to revise and improve the interview guide. The research to interview question alignment is described in Table 3 below. The field test of the email instrument has been completed.

Credibility and Transferability

Credibility is the qualitative counterpart to internal validity (Rose & Johnson, 2020). According to Merriam and Tisdell (2015), credibility pertains to the internal coherence of the study. Credibility has been achieved in several important ways for the current research study. Transferability is provided through descriptions and contextspecific social media behaviors and interactions that are explored, interpreted, and documented across diverse small, microenterprise businesses and consumers. The key components of the study have been carefully aligned to ensure that instruments and processes are aligned and stem from the problem statement and research questions. The study included several validating steps in the analysis.

The alignment served to ensure that the data collected for this study addressed the original research problem. Use of source data triangulation from interviews, social media content and business documentation, should support credibility (Rose & Johnson, 2020). Member checking or verifying that the person interview does fall into this group, has been employed to ensure the correctness of data collected from the owner and employee interviews. The member checking also included a follow-up conversation with both the business owner and employees and providing online questions through SurveyMonkey for customers.

Transferability corresponds to external validity (Rose & Johnson, 2020). However, qualitative results cannot be generalized (Merriam & Tisdell, 2015). Instead, the goal was to carefully document the study so readers can determine if the results may be transferred to similar settings. Transferability also provides information gained during the research process to other study settings, participant responses, interpretations, and behaviors for example, of questions provided to the subjects.

Data Collection

Data collection for the research study proceeded as follows. Businesses were identified through public venues such as Chambers of Commerce, business directories, or their social media sites. Field-testing of the interview questions and any questionnaires occurred prior to IRB approval. Prior to recruiting any participants or collecting any data, IRB approval was obtained through the University of Phoenix IRB office. No data was collected prior to obtaining both IRB approval and site authorizations.

As a preliminary step upon receiving study approval, the five businesses were selected and contacted to receive permission to use their permission to conduct the research (see Appendix F) as necessary. Once site permissions were obtained, the primary participants, the business owners, signed permission documents. Business owners were contacted in-person or via email, with a recruitment message that detailed the study, its purpose, and who was eligible to participate. Participants reviewed informed consent information in-person or electronically provided via email, they personally or electronically accepted the informed consent forms.

Once informed consent was accepted, an interview was offered to each microenterprise owner. If available time for an in-person interview was problematic, data collection occurred using an email instrument to provide the questions and data capture. No identifiers of participant information were utilized for data coding, rather, a letter or number was used to denote the participant. The interviewee may have known that other business owners were providing information concerning their use of social media for research, but as the businesses were all in distinct markets, this notion did not influence interview results. In-person interviews, if conducted were video and audio recorded and then transcribed and provided to participants for validation and checking. Data collection sources are identified in Table 3.

The observation protocol utilized during the collection process was an unstructured and participant observation method providing for flexibility and allowing for detailed narrative observations. The focus of the protocol was to capture observationally relevant information about each microenterprise. Using this systematic approach, Printed and Published information were reviewed through local paper ads or posted placards in the business local, or communities. Observations consisted of informal in-person visits to each of the microenterprises to converse with the business owner. Each business website was visited to examine products and services listed, except for the repairperson who did not have a website. A further review of comments was also conducted on the major social media sites such as Facebook and TikTok for each business. These observations were utilized in addition to the email instruments that were distributed to each participant for completion.

Once they completed the email instruments, participants were asked about their availability for any follow-up data collection that may be required. Each business owner was asked if it was acceptable to request interviews with their employees and were provided with written and electronic versions of the consent forms via email for the employees to fill out. At least one employee from each business was recruited (see Appendix A) for the employee interview.

As stated, employee participants were provided with separate interview-based informed consent forms after acknowledging their interest in providing interview feedback to the researcher. For each of the businesses, time became an obstacle, and an online email instrument was utilized containing the same questions as the in-person interviews were provided. The study researcher acted as a moderator for any of the informal conversations. Each of the participants were provided with a copy of the transcript of their responses only, to review and correct as desired.

Customers' responses were captured through SurveyMonkey, with the survey containing questions relating to the customers' social media experiences. Flyers were posted in each business with a QR code and web link to the survey. Before starting the survey, a description of the survey, the focus of the survey, the expected time to complete and an assurance that no identifiable personal information was captured, was stated. An acceptance or refusal button option was provided that was pressed before the survey questions are presented, providing the ability of the participant to exit before starting the survey. If the customer consents, it was with the understanding that all customer confidentiality was maintained, and no customer information was captured other than responses to the survey questions.

During the data collection process, no names, or identifiers were used; rather, alphanumeric coded references for each data object was stored. Alphanumeric codes represented all data objects. Upon completion of the study, all collected data and audio that was electronic in nature was then encrypted and stored on two devices: the recording computer and a USB flash drive that was then stored in a controlled, locked environment.

Data Analysis

Data analysis included thematic analysis and case study triangulation of two other data sources. The supplemental data sources included internet web site comment reviews and social media application artifacts such as information and reviews found on Facebook and Instagram. Initial data tagging was attempted using NVivo 15 qualitative data analysis software but deemed to compute intensive considering the small data sets, further tagging was competed by hand using Microsoft Word 2016. Another valuable source of information was informal conversations had with each microenterprise owner, as Swain and King (2022) indicates.

The coding goal is to develop themes (Braun & Clarke, 2022). Developing themes involve examining the codes, labels and connections within the captured data that form larger ideas or categories, a process called axial coding (Lim, 2025). The more significant ideas or connections represented themes. These patterns or observations supported forming themes which then supported evidence to the research questions. The specific coding and analysis process followed the Braun and Clarke (2022) thematic analysis model. Coding of collected data followed ethical and accuracy guidelines and was sorted on response lines and keywords.

The transcription process of each survey and email instrument allowed for the opportunity to become familiar with the data, the first phase of the thematic approach. The second phase is generating initial tags that included checking and rechecking responses and building a source file that was imported into NVivo. During this step, each item of note was assigned a tag and a color in the NVivo software, identifying interesting parts of the information such as “easy to use” or “supports the business”. The next step in the thematic analysis involved searching for themes, as Braun and Clarke (2022), indicated. The selection of key ideas found in the data was developed by the researcher to begin clustering of tags and then code building the foundation for themes. These codes reflected the key ideas in the data and areas of interest supporting the themes. Axial coding, drawing connections between the concepts/issues, refining, and situating them within a category or code, as indicated by Lim (2025), was part of the theme process.

The tagged and coded data supported the theme foundation and focused on how often and where the data occurred and providing insight and importance to that information. Before theme naming, any incomplete or duplicate themes were merged into others. The substantiated themes were then refined, defined, and named (Braun & Clarke, 2022). The defined and named themes supported the building of a compelling story. Additionally in this step, a table of evidence or codebook, Figure 5, was developed documenting quotes from participants and the ideas that supported each theme.

Figure 5

Perceived Mattering Codebook Example

Theme	Sub-Themes	Definitions	Examples from Transcripts
Owners Reasons and Perceptions for Implementing Social Media		Reasons for use	I really enjoyed using these platforms to communicate with other users
Cobbler 1A		Kinds of Social Media Use	With Facebook I found it had a wide audience and was much easier to use and set up a personal profile. Google Business Yelp, Instagram
		Perceptions for Implementation	platforms are free of charge to use, my time is the number one resource. Initially setting up the content, maintaining the content to keep all information current and relevant require time and effort usually done, by me, outside of my shop hours
Florist 1B		Reasons for use	A way to reach a large audience.
		Kinds of Social Media Use	Facebook and Instagram
		Perceptions for Implementation	We realized that it is important for a Google rating to access social media as a way of advertising

Note. Figure 5 describes an example of the codebook contents (Wieland, 2025)

Coding of collected data followed ethical and accuracy guidelines and was sorted on response lines and keywords. The transcription process allows for the ability to become familiar with the data (Lester et al., 2020). Since the sample size of businesses was small, a manual replication of responses to all conversations, online surveys, and any other cues such during in person interactions and such were noted. The NVivo 15 software was abandoned due to the small sample size and intense compute constraints, and manual coding was completed using Microsoft Word. Each response item of note provided a letter based on the participant responding, and tracked through question responses (see Appendix G, H, I).

Once the three diverse sources of data were analyzed using thematic analysis, the data was triangulated. Triangulation involves combining the results of at least two other data sources (Yin, 2017). As such, the results were compared, and points of agreement or disagreement were noted. Points of agreement strengthen the results. On the other hand, points of disagreement represent areas in need of further research. The final step was to compile a report (Braun & Clarke, 2022). The report has been presented in Chapter 4.

Chapter Summary

In summary, the purpose of this qualitative exploratory multiple case study was to explore the perceptions of owners, employees, and customers on the influence of social media on microenterprise family-owned businesses in the Delaware, Maryland, and Virginia (DELMARVA) region.. To address this purpose, a qualitative exploratory multiple case study was conducted. The study was guided by three research questions: (a)

What are the owner perceptions of owners at family-owned microenterprises in the

DELMARVA region regarding their reasons for implementing social media strategies.

(b) What are the employees' perceptions at family-owned microenterprises in the

DELMARVA region regarding the influence on customers concerning the business's social media strategies and (c) What are the customers' perceptions of family-owned microenterprises in the DELMARVA region regarding the accuracy and usability of the social media interfaces.

In this case, the study population consisted of five microenterprise owners, employees, and business customers in the DELMARVA region. Microenterprises are the smallest category of small businesses, those with 1-20 employees (Handayani, 2023). The participant criteria required that the microenterprises be family-owned businesses with revenues of less than five million dollars. Within this overall population, the target population was family-owned microenterprise owners and employees in a transient DELMARVA region. A purposive criterion sampling technique was used to explain, as Nyimbili and Nyimbili (2024) indicated the specific criterion that each business was a microenterprise.

The sample included five business owners and five employees. Data collection for the study involved multiple data sources. The owner or designate from each business participated in an individual interview, or if time for the in-person interview was not available the data were collected via email. The observation protocol utilized during the collection process was an unstructured and participant observation method providing for flexibility and allowing for detailed narrative observations. The focus of the protocol was capturing observationally relevant information about each microenterprise using this systematic approach.

Additionally, an employee from each of the five businesses was interviewed, upon consent and confidentiality signatures. The option of email data collection was provided if time for an in-person interview was problematic. Additional data were observed and gathered from the businesses' social media pages and online customer surveys. An interview guide and script led the interview process. Data analysis for the research study included qualitative thematic analysis and case study triangulation. Customer surveys were conducted using SurveyMonkey as the primary data collection source.

Chapter 4

Analysis and Results

The purpose of this qualitative exploratory multiple case study was to explore the perceptions of owners and employees and customers at family-owned microenterprises in Delaware, Maryland, and Virginia, or the DELMARVA region. In Chapter 4, focus is on analyzing business owner reasons for implementing social media strategies, the success of those strategies, and the challenges faced in using those strategies. A qualitative research method was adopted for conducting the research study. Qualitative methodology aligns with the current research study for a series of key reasons.

The research study aligns with and was grounded in qualitative research, characterized by its open-ended, inductive, and contextually rich approach. The primary objective of the study was to examine the perceptions of owners and employees within family-owned microenterprises in the DELMARVA region concerning the motivations for adopting social media strategies. The study aimed to achieve a comprehensive understanding of the perceptions held by owners and employees by examining both the success of selected social media strategies and the challenges associated with their implementation.

Additionally, the customers' perspective of the usability of these technologies was evaluated. The difference between the strategic intentions of business owners and the practical utility experienced by customers represents a critical analytical dimension, with conclusions drawn from these distinctions presented in the data analysis section of Chapter 4. Given the exploratory nature of this research, a multiple case study design was employed as an approach that was particularly well-suited for investigating emerging and underexplored topics. An exploratory multiple case study provided a foundational understanding of the central research phenomenon, facilitating deeper inquiry into its complexities.

The research process and data analysis described in Chapter 4 consists of a thorough review of the interview surveys and transcripts, resulting in a summary of the keywords or elements of each interview and survey. Data from the interview and email instruments was coded using techniques based on Braun and Clark (2023). The process involved identifying recurring themes or patterns and linking them to the research objectives. The analysis examined factors influencing small business owners' thoughts and motivations regarding social media use, thereby supporting the resolution of the research questions. Additionally, second-party data were captured through observations and interpretations using the observations protocol defined earlier.

Research Questions

A primary objective of the current qualitative exploratory multiple case study was to investigate the multifaceted rationale behind small family-operated business owners' decisions to implement social media marketing. By integrating rigorous qualitative methodologies with theoretical frameworks from digital marketing and organizational decision-making, this research seeks to identify both the explicit and nuanced features that drive these businesses to strategically leverage social media platforms. Another objective was to evaluate the successes and failures of microenterprise marketing initiatives. A further aim was to analyze the challenges inherent in implementing these marketing strategies.

To address these research imperatives comprehensively, the study was guided by three research questions:

R1: What are the owner perceptions of family-owned microenterprises in the

DELMARVA region regarding their reasons for implementing social media strategies?

R2: What are the employee perceptions of family-owned microenterprises in the DELMARVA region regarding the influence of customers on business social media strategies?

R3: What are the customer perceptions of family-owned microenterprises in the

DELMARVA region regarding the accuracy and usability of the social media interfaces?

Data Collection

Once the University of Phoenix Institutional Review Board approved the research study, the research began. Purposive criterion based sampling was used to recruit microenterprises in the identified Baltimore area. The recruitment process and inclusion criteria consisted of an internet search of locally family-owned small businesses in the DELMARVA region, with five or less employees, less than five million dollars in revenue and more specifically the southern areas of Baltimore and surrounding counties. Driving through local communities also provided insight into potential research subjects where several small family-owned businesses were identified.

Once the business owners expressed an interest in participating in the research, the business owners were sent a follow-up email requesting an in-person meeting time, and in that email, an Informed Consent form was provided for the owner to complete. When the meeting time was determined and arranged, the researcher met with the business owner and described the purpose of the qualitative exploratory multiple case study was discussed. During an in-person meeting, the consent process was continuously emphasized that participation was strictly voluntary, and that confidentiality would be strictly maintained and adhered to. The consent process also indicated that if the subject wished to withdraw from the study, they could do so at any time and for any reason. This proved fortuitous as two of the original seven microenterprises dropped out later in the process, leaving the required five businesses for the research.

The ethical considerations, including confidentiality and informed consent, as a rule were strictly adhered to when handling sensitive participant data. Although the study had a small sample size of five microenterprises, the group of businesses represented a diverse subset of microenterprises that dot the Southern Baltimore business landscape within the DELMARVA region, as well as representing a range of newer and older, more established businesses.

Five participant owners and five employees were selected to participate by ZOOM or in-person meetings, or if unavailable for a ZOOM or in-person meeting, an email instrument was used to capture the data. Unfortunately, due to significant scheduling issues all five owners and employees selected to participate via the email instrument. Each email was sent solely to each participant and to a personal email account with intended use verbiage. The researcher also assured all the participants of data and personal confidentiality via the email instrument. The email instrument contained the same set of questions used during the ZOOM interviews to maintain consistency across data collection methods and was kept confidential via separation of data and forms by using personal email addresses with intended use.

To obtain responses from business customers, a flyer was posted in each business with a QR code and web link information that pointed to the SurveyMonkey platform where the customer survey were conducted. Within the customer survey the informed consent was embedded as an introductory component of the process. The survey data were collected via the SurveyMonkey export process and stored on the personal hard drive of the researcher. This data upon completion of the research will be transferred to a USB drive and locked away at the researcher's house. The USB and any paper documents will be destroyed after three years.

Responses to survey questions constituted a critical data source for this qualitative exploratory multiple case study, providing insight into participants' perceptions, attitudes, and experiences. The reliability and validity of these responses were contingent upon both the clarity of the survey instrument and the respondents' comprehension and willingness to engage authentically. Analyzing these replies involved not only identifying patterns and trends but also accounting for potential biases, including social desirability bias, non-response bias, and acquiescence bias. Careful interpretation of survey data was essential to ensure that the findings accurately reflected the underlying constructs under investigation and contributed meaningfully to the research objectives.

As a follow up to the email instrument capture, and serving as artifact collection, short informal in person conversations were conducted between owners, employee, and the researcher. The researcher served as the moderator for each of these informal conversations, ensuring consistency in the interview process. During each informal conversation, notes were taken and then transcribed by copying notes into tags and then into codes and if appropriate built into the codebook, ensuring to anonymize participant identities, company names, and any other identifiable information.

Data Collection Process

The data collection process consisted of, and email instrument containing seven questions for employees and eight questions for owners and focused on capturing information about the participant's experiences and perceptions of social media use. Additional information concerning the business owner's implementation of social media, and the employee's perception on the influences of use of social media by customers were also captured. During the online survey for customers, perceptions of the accuracy and usability of businesses' social media interfaces constituted the primary focus, but also the ease of use and importance of the microenterprise social media presence were ascertained.

After the data from surveys and email instruments were collected, the researcher transcribed and coded the microenterprises as A through E. Secondary demographic data and responses were coded to identify any nuances that may have been missed during the short informal conversations, such as body language or vocal changes to denote feelings. Notes that were taken during those informal conversations were added to the transcription to provide a robust picture of collected data.

A copy of the transcribed notes was sent to each participant for verification and approval, however if no response for changes was provided within two weeks, the data were used as is. All the transcribed data is kept secure without any identifiers or names and after review and approval by the participants and all original recorded data was deleted, and any notes and paperwork has been digitally scanned and then destroyed. The scanned data has been moved from the researcher's computer to a password protected on an encrypted USB flash drive, which will remain stored in a lock box in the researcher's home for three years. After the three-year period is up, the USB drive will be physically destroyed.

Business Demographics

The business demographics consisted of five small microenterprise business owners, five employees, and several customers in this transient area within the DELMARVA states, which includes Delaware, Maryland, and

Virginia. The research focused on businesses in the Southern Baltimore region. Included in the study sample group was the business owner, a business employee, and several business customers. Any interview participant could be of any race, or sex, but must be at least 18 years of age. The researcher collected demographic data as an important artifact.

Microenterprises are the smallest category of small businesses and consist of those businesses with less than 10 employees. Participants in the study were chosen from a list of small, or microenterprise, family-owned, businesses with research focusing on social media implementation and customer interaction information. Incidental owner information observed was three of the five business owners were female, ages 18-69; two were males between the ages 18-69. Each participant owned the business for greater than two years and with one owning the business for over 30 years, two owned their business for less than five years and two businesses owned for more than 10 years but less than 20.

Table 3 summarizes some of the initial demographic data from the businesses' owners within the research study such as gender, age range and years of experience:

Table 3

Business Owner Demographic Information for Selected Microenterprises

Business	Gender	Age Range	Years of Experience
BO 1A	M	18-69	30+
BO 1B	F	18-69	>20
BO 1C	M	18-69	<=5
BO 1D	F	18-69	<10
BO 1E	F	18-69	<5

Note. Table 3 provides business owner demographic breakout (Wieland, 2024)

Table 4 summarizes some of the initial demographic data gathered from the employees of the businesses.

Table 4

Business Employee Demographic Information for Selected Microenterprises

Business	Gender	Age Range	Years as Employee
E 1A	M	18-69	>5
E 1B	F	18-69	>5
E 1C	M	18-69	<5
E 1D	M	18-69	>5
E 1E	M	18-69	<5

Note. Table 4 provides business employee demographic breakout (Wieland, 2024)

During the interview and survey process, participants were encouraged to provide any lived experience or perceptions concerning the research subject. Transcribing data collected was a critical step in qualitative research, ensuring accuracy, consistency, and reliability in subsequent analysis. Email instrument responses were captured and then transcribed, high-quality transcription demanded meticulous attention to detail, including verbatim capture of spoken dialogue, nonverbal cues where relevant, and contextual annotations to preserve meaning.

Table 5 provides additional types of demographic information about these businesses:

Table 5

Location and Business Type Information for Microenterprises

Business	Location	Years in Business	Products
1A	South Baltimore	30+	Cobbler
1B	Pasadena MD	>20	Florist
1C	Pasadena MD	<=5	Handyman
1D	Glen Burnie MD	<10	Marketing/Analytics
1E	Pasadena MD	<5	Merchant

Note. Table 5 provides business type breakout (Wieland, 2024)

Data Analysis

The data analysis for the present qualitative multiple case study employed Braun and Clarkes (2022) qualitative thematic analysis in conjunction with case study triangulation. In the context of this research, case study triangulation was achieved through the integration of multiple data sources, including interviews, web site and social media reviews. These additional sources were included in the data file. The codebook observations made during the informal conversations also included in the data file, and surveys, to enhance the credibility of findings and mitigate any potential research bias.

The qualitative exploratory multiple case study design was implemented through four distinct stages: (a) identification and recruitment of potential participants, (b) execution of the interview process, (c) review of relevant documents and publicly accessible online data that were reviewed for comments included in the data file, and (d) transcription and analysis of collected data.

The first stage of the data analysis process was the distribution of the data collection process. An email instrument was used to conduct data collection for all five owners and employees. This email instrument included a Microsoft Word document containing questions for each participant to respond to and elaborate on. Additionally, customer surveys were conveniently distributed within each business via paper flyer containing the survey QR code or web link to a SurveyMonkey online survey, and the resulting responses served as an essential component of the study. The customer collected data offered an anonymous perspective from the customer population of social media use.

The data collected in the participant responses were analyzed to identify data that supports the research questions, the perceptions, and reasons for implementing social media by ownership, the perceptions of employees concerning the influence of social media marketing and customer perceptions of the usability of social media tools and technology. Analysis of the collected data supported the analytical thematic process and was hand coded using Microsoft Word performed by the researcher.

Coding

Following the coding process, as indicated by Braun and Clarke (2022) the first step was to become familiar with the data. All collected data was compiled into three separate files, one for each subject type, owners, employee and customer responses. The next step was to identify and generate initial codes, where recurring words and phrases were identified and assigned a specific color, as seen in Figure 6. The next step was to search for recurring or commonly used words and phrases and assign initial codes to these clusters. The next step was to review these themes for coherence and determine if there was enough meaningful data to support the theme. Microsoft Word clouds were constructed at this point to visually support the themes. Naming the theme was the next step and this provided focus and connected to the research questions. The final step is producing the report.

Figure 6

Coding Words and Phrases

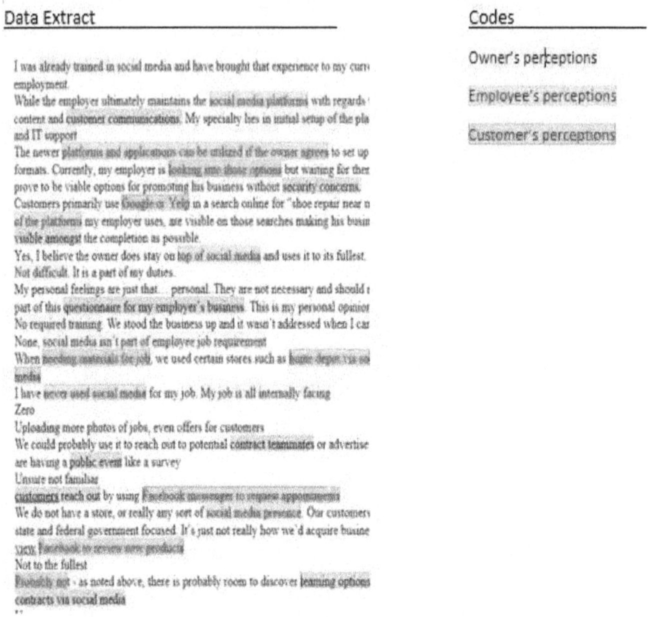

Data Extract	Codes
I was already trained in social media and have brought that experience to my curr	Owner's perceptions
employment.	Employee's perceptions
While the employer ultimately maintains the social media platforms with regards	Customer's perceptions

content and customer communications. My specialty lies in initial setup of the pla
and IT support
The newer platforms and applications can be utilized if the owner agrees to set up
formats. Currently, my employer is looking into those options but waiting for ther
prove to be viable options for promoting his business without security concerns.
Customers primarily use Google or Yelp in a search online for "shoe repair near n
of the platforms my employer uses, are visible on those searches making his busin
visible amongst the completion as possible.
Yes, I believe the owner does stay on top of social media and uses it to its fullest.
Not difficult. It is a part of my duties.
My personal feelings are just that... personal. They are not necessary and should
part of this questionnaire for my employer's business. This is my personal opinion
No required training. We stood the business up and it wasn't addressed when I car
None, social media isn't part of employee job requirement
When needing materials for job, we used certain stores such as home depot via so
media
I have never used social media for my job. My job is all internally facing
Zero
Uploading more photos of jobs, even offers for customers
We could probably use it to reach out to potential contract teammates or advertise
are having a public event like a survey
Unsure not familiar
customers reach out by using Facebook messenger to request appointments
We do not have a store, or really any sort of social media presence. Our customers
state and federal government focused. It's just not really how we'd acquire busine
view Facebook to review new products
Not to the fullest
Possibly not - as noted above, there is probably room to discover learning options
contracts via social media

Note. Figure 6 describes an example of the recurring words and phrases in captured data.

The coding process of the data analysis was qualitative data analysis software for data tagging and then implemented Microsoft Word for more detailed coding and codebook creation, Figure 7. This part of the analysis was completed by Microsoft Word including the coding of the primary, first-party data collected and secondary data collection sources. The coding and initial analysis followed all ethical and accuracy guidelines, and the data was sorted using response lines and keywords. A partial example of data contained within the Perceived Mattering codebook is provided in Figure 7 as a representation of the codebook.

Figure 7

Perceived Mattering Codebook Example

Theme	Sub-Themes	Definitions	Examples from Transcripts
Owners Reasons and Perceptions for Implementing Social Media		Reasons for use	I really enjoyed using these platforms to communicate with other users
Cobbler 1A		Kinds of Social Media Use	With Facebook I found it had a wide audience and was much easier to use and set up a personal profile. Google Business Yelp, Instagram
		Perceptions for Implementation	platforms are free of charge to use, my time is the number one resource. Initially setting up the content, maintaining the content to keep all information current and relevant require time and effort usually done, by me, outside of my shop hours
Florist 1B		Reasons for use	A way to reach a large audience.
		Kinds of Social Media Use	Facebook and Instagram
		Perceptions for Implementation	We realized that it is important for a Google rating to access social media as a way of advertising

Note. Figure 7 describes an example of the codebook contents (Wieland, 2025)

The initial process was to bring the collected data together. A significant part of the process was the completed and transcribed research files. This process facilitated the construction of word clouds, thereby enabling a more visually prominent and analytically accessible representation of the collected qualitative data (see Figures 8, 9 and 10). Microsoft Word codebook creation supported the forming of connections between transcript examples and emerging themes. These themes represent connections between the results participants provided and the original research questions posed as the foundation for the study.

Microsoft Word facilitated a more immersive review of the data and the development of emergent themes. Microsoft Word, although not designed to provide a robust platform for managing and analyzing large volumes of qualitative data, does support the enabling of triangulation of the findings through advanced search functions and visualizations. Microsoft Word also proved to be easy to use within the data sets and provide accurate representations of the data.

The compiled data presented a supporting framework of the initial themes consisting of the reason for social media use and ease of implementation, the influence of social media and the usability of social media tools. The results of the study are important, as the knowledge captured may contribute some information, ease of use and commonly used applications for example, of significance to the field of study. This information may also add value and perspective to small businesses who may be entertaining the idea of implementing social media as a marketing tool and the phenomenon studied.

The findings of the study revealed recurring keywords and contextual patterns that aligned with and directly aligned with the research questions. The application of a word-based analytical approach facilitated a deeper understanding of participants' perspectives and experiences regarding the utilization of social media within the microenterprise environment. This method enabled the identification of salient themes, providing valuable insight into the ways participants perceive and engage with social media as part of their business operations.

Results

Social media, as an online consumer-driven platform, has evolved significantly over the past decade, fundamentally transforming the processes by which products and services are marketed, purchased, and consumed. This technological evolution has had a profound impact on consumer-business interactions, influencing engagement strategies across businesses of all sizes. Furthermore, the integration of social media into commercial practices has facilitated near real-time availability and delivery of goods and services in numerous sectors, enhancing both consumer convenience and business responsiveness.

Social media has been found to support both significant growth and increased revenues for microenterprises, and this phenomenon, the researcher found, can be directly attributed to increased social media's impact on business awareness and availability. Microenterprises have a greater incentive to improve financial and competitive positions, as family-owned microenterprises typically have significant professional and personal investments in the success of the business. There was a distinction between consumer use or utility of social media, business strategy in deploying social media technologies and using social media as a marketing tool. This technology may be viewed as the immediate practicality for the microenterprise owner versus long-term goals and strategy that is immediate application of the tools versus a long-term project. Social media technologies, as the microenterprise owners found, were an excellent tool, but did not provide all the answers to economic issues that surround the small business owner. Table 6 provides the connection between the research questions and themes found during the analysis.

Table 6

Research Question to Theme Connection

Research Question	Theme Association
R1 What are the owner perceptions of family-owned microenterprises in the DELMARVA region regarding their reasons for implementing social media strategies?	**Theme 1:** The Owner's Reasons and Perceptions for Implementing Social Media
R2 What are the employee perceptions of family-owned microenterprises in the DELMARVA region regarding the influence of customers on business social media strategies?	**Theme 2:** The Employee's Perceptions of the Influence of Social Media Marketing
R3 What are the customer perceptions of family-owned microenterprises in the DELMARVA region regarding the accuracy and usability of the social media interfaces?	**Theme 3:** The Customer's Perceptions of Usability of Social Media Tools

Note. Table 6 denotes the connection between the research and interview questions

(Wieland, 2024)

Theme 1: The Owner Reasons and Perceptions for Implementing Social Media

Discovered during the study after transcribing data collected, the owners of these five microenterprises indicated that the main reason and perception for implementing social media long-term, was that technology was a critical component for small businesses aiming to compete in a complex and crowded marketplace. Data results for business owners are provided in Appendix G. Business owner BO 1E offered a reason to use the technology "ease of use and to target our demographics".

The technology offered a cost-effective, highly targeted, and engagement-focused advertising strategy for the small, local family-owned microenterprise. Business owner BO 1A stated, "when Facebook started offering business pages, I just wanted to get the word out, and it was easy and simple to do". The ease of implementing a Facebook page requires limited effort and knowledge. Other forms of social media such as web page interaction was a bit more difficult and in some instances required support from outside of the business.

For the microenterprise, often operating within limited budgets, social media presents a platform where they can maximize consumer reach and impact without the excessive costs associated with traditional advertising. Through targeted advertising features on platforms like Facebook, Instagram, and LinkedIn, businesses can target specific demographics that align with their customer base, which was particularly valuable in local markets. Business owner BO 1C stated, "At the beginning of the opening of the business I started a business page and shared it with my friends". This was an example where social media enables direct interaction with customers, fostering a sense of community and brand loyalty that was harder to achieve through other channels.

Social media has emerged as a highly effective and indispensable marketing tool for small businesses. This is primarily due to its ability to foster direct engagement with a highly targeted audience at a fraction of the cost of traditional advertising methods, as BO 1C states "I don't pay Facebook for advertising", "Facebook was free and easy to reach potential clients, Angie's list helped me get new clients". The study research subjects found social platforms such as Facebook, Instagram, and LinkedIn, providing small businesses with the opportunity to build brand visibility, engage in meaningful interactions, and drive customer loyalty with personalized content. These platforms leverage advanced technologies that enable precise demographic and behavioral targeting, allowing small businesses to reach potential customers with greater accuracy and efficiency. The perceptions of social media as an excellent marketing tool by participant microenterprise owners adheres to the original question of one of the reasons to implement social media. Moreover, the real-time feedback and data capabilities available within social media facilitate the optimization of marketing strategies, making it easier for small enterprises to adapt quickly to market trends and consumer preferences. Consequently, social media not only makes access to marketing resources easy to use but also enables the microenterprise to scale effectively within the increasingly digital economy.

This interaction also allows for real-time feedback, which can be invaluable for refining products or services to meet customer needs more precisely. The research indicated significant preferences for social media applications that the different microenterprises implemented including Facebook, Instagram, websites and other social media presences. The goal of most small, microenterprise businesses was to attract customers, increase revenues and grow the brand name.

Another perception of business owners was that social media technology has proven to be an accessible, easy-to-use, and user-friendly tool for microenterprise owners, offering an intuitive interface that requires minimal technical expertise. Platforms such as Instagram, Facebook, and Twitter provide straightforward, easy content creation. Business owner BO C1 states, "social media has been very easy and very rewarding. Happy customers will share experiences and new client see". Scheduling and analytic tools can also empower even the most technologically inexperienced entrepreneurs to engage with their target audiences effectively. These platforms offer user-friendly features, such as drag-and-drop content design, automated posting schedules, and real-time performance metrics, allowing microenterprise owners to manage their marketing efforts with ease. As business owner BO B1 states "social media is a way to reach a large audience using Facebook and Instagram". Additionally, the lowcost nature of social media tools, combined with their wide reach and brand creation possibilities, ensures that even small-scale operators can access marketing capabilities without the need for substantial financial investment or advanced technical knowledge. Business owner BO E1 indicates, "during initial social media implementation there was trial and error". There are extensive online communities and tutorial resources available for social media platforms that allow microenterprise owners to acquire quickly the skills necessary for maximizing their presence, positioning social media technology as an indispensable, easy-to-use solution for small-scale business growth.

Appendix G provides background on the multifaceted nature of these microenterprise business owners, where considerations of time, budget constraints, and the alignment of social media goals with broader business objectives are key factors in shaping social media strategies. The number of years in business and the type of business provided insight to use and perceptions as well. In an increasingly digital economy, this table acts as a vital resource for both academic inquiry and practical guidance, helping to bridge the gap between theoretical frameworks and the lived experiences of small business owners in the digital age. Appendix G also provides insight into the diversity and strategy of applications used. The table describes the microenterprise owner (BO) and business types (A1, B1, C1, D1, E1) as points of reference for data analysis.

The findings derived from the owner responses indicate that Facebook emerged as the most accessible and user-friendly platform for initiating a social media presence. Establishing a Facebook business page represented the most straightforward and commonly adopted strategy among the small businesses surveyed. Business owner BO E1 states, "social media provides the benefit of gaining customers and expanding sales reach". This observation is further supported by the word cloud generated from owner responses, which highlights the prominence of Facebook as a preferred platform for engaging with customers and promoting business activities.

Key terms such as “business,” “social media,” and “Facebook” indicate a primary focus on leveraging social media for business expansion and customer engagement. Additionally, the presence of words like “page,” “use,” and “contracts” suggests that resource allocation and effective planning remain central concerns. This qualitative representation underscores the critical areas where business owners seek guidance, highlighting the intersection of digital marketing aspirations and operational constraints in the small business landscape. The word cloud represented in Figure 8 provides a visual analysis of the predominant themes in small business owner responses to social mediarelated inquiries, offering insight into their strategic priorities and challenges.

Figure 8

Microenterprise Owner Social Media Word Cloud

Note. Figure 8 provides a visual summary of business owner perceptions (Wieland, 2025)

For small businesses, the connection can translate into organic growth, as satisfied customers are likely to share content or recommend products to other social media users, amplifying the business' reach and credibility. Business owner D stated, "So far customer response has been very positive and with little to no effort, people are signing up for classes and introduction calls". By establishing a strong social media presence, small businesses can not only drive customer acquisition and retention but also enhance brand awareness, position themselves as competitive leaders, and adapt to market trends with agility. In a digital-first economy, social media marketing was no longer optional but essential for small businesses aiming to thrive and grow.

Theme 2: The Employee Perceptions of the Influence of Social Media Marketing

The study found that the influence social media has on consumers finding and visiting small businesses was significant. Social media has profoundly influenced consumer behavior in discovering and engaging with small businesses, reshaping the traditional customer journey from initial awareness to in-store or online visits. The algorithms on platforms like Facebook, Instagram, and TikTok enable businesses to reach audiences who align with their ideal customer profiles, placing them directly in front of users who might not have otherwise encountered them. Social media's role as a discovery tool was significant, with location-based features, hashtags, and paid promotions allowing consumers to find easily businesses within their vicinity or in specific niches of interest.

Employees in many situations play a key role in the utilization of social media to support the small microenterprise businesses, serving as both content creators and facilitators of online engagement. The contributions of employees often include generating and sharing promotional content, responding to customer inquiries, and monitoring online feedback, all of which enhance the business's digital presence. Little, if any training was required on social media applications as most employees use several outside of the business environment. One employee, E 1A stated "I was already trained in social media and have brought that experience to my employer".

Found in the research; however, is that some employees were less connected with the business social media presences as described by an employee for business E 1D stating, "I have never used social media for my job. My job is all internally facing". This identifies that there are circumstances, even for microenterprises, where the use of social media or smart phone technologies generally do not fit into normal employee customer interactions, where the employee works internally to the company in a non-customer facing position. This could be a teaching moment, or an area where employee training might be helpful, where the owner could work with the employee to enhance the capabilities of business staff.

Appendix H represents a structured analysis of employee's responses to key social media inquiries, offering insights into their strategic approaches, challenges, and engagement tactics. The data revealed patterns of business use, training and personal feelings on the interaction, and perceived effectiveness of various platforms, highlighting both opportunities and constraints in digital marketing efforts. Notably, the responses underscore a divergence in confidence levels, with a number of employees demonstrating adeptness in leveraging social media for business visibility, while others express uncertainty regarding best practices. The analysis contributed to a broader understanding of how small businesses employees navigate the evolving digital landscape from a business perspective.

The use of social media by employees depends on the business environment and level of customer interaction. Effective use of social media by employees can amplify the microenterprise brand visibility and foster customer relationships, and contribute to the overall competitiveness of the microenterprise within the digital marketplace. The employee can be an integral part of the social media customer interaction puzzle, where they may be the first ones to greet a customer at the business front door. The employee can steer the customer to products they may be interested in. Employees may not be fully engaging in the marketing efforts of the microenterprise owner. Employees provide a significant presence between ownership and customers, where informal discussions between the employee and a customer may be greatly beneficial in identifying gaps in use of the technology and newer applications that customers are using to locate businesses.

Key terms such as “social media,” “business,” and “job” suggest a focus on interactive customer relationships and strategic messaging. The prominence of words related to challenges, such as “platforms” and “options,” further highlights common constraints employees face in executing social media strategies effectively. This visualization serves as a qualitative tool for identifying patterns in employee perspectives, thereby informing best practices and potential areas for organizational support and training.

By capturing these recurring themes, the word cloud served as a qualitative tool for identifying patterns in employee perspectives, thereby informing best practices and potential areas for organizational support and training. The word cloud visualization contributed to a more nuanced comprehension of how employees navigate the complexities of social media engagement within the constraints of small business environments, offering a foundation for strategic improvements in digital communication practices. The word cloud in Figure 9 provides a visual representation of the most frequently occurring terms in employee responses to small business social media inquiries, offering valuable visual insights into prevailing themes and concerns. Figure 9 denotes the microenterprise employees' use of social media for business purposes and to further customer interactions. It must be noted that employee interaction with social media were less connected to business social media than the owners.

Figure 9

Microenterprise Employee Social Media Word Cloud

Note. Figure 9 provides a visual summary of employees' perceptions (Wieland, 2025)

The employee use of social media within small microenterprise businesses can be pivotal, facilitating brand awareness, customer engagement, and market expansion. Given the resource constraints inherent in microenterprises, the employee can often assume multifaceted roles, integrating social media responsibilities with core operational tasks. Employee engagement in digital platforms extends beyond content review and competitor information; it encompasses real-time customer interaction, reputation management, and the cultivation of an online presence that aligns with the businesses overarching goals and objectives. Addressing knowledge barriers through targeted skill development initiatives, structured content strategies, and the integration of automation tools can enhance the employee efficacy in leveraging social media as a cost-effective marketing instrument.

Consequently, empowering employees with the necessary competencies and resources not only strengthens the business digital footprint and contributes to its long-term sustainability in an increasingly competitive marketplace.

Theme 3: The Customer Perception of the Usability of Social Media Tools

One of the issues investigated during the research involved usability, or userfriendly issues navigating social media as an online consumer-based medium. The rapid adoption of social media as a consumer-oriented platform has introduced notable usability issues that could influence the user experience and, subsequently, consumer trust and engagement. One significant issue was the inconsistency in design and navigation across various platforms that can create confusion and disrupt the user journey. Social media design inconsistency affects consumers who must adapt to disparate layouts, interface structures, and content presentation styles, depending on the platform they are using. However, customer interaction with social media plays a significant role in business successes or failures.

By interacting with content through likes, shares, comments, and reviews, customers can contribute to reach and brand credibility, amplifying the business's presence beyond its immediate consumer network. User-generated content, such as testimonials, product reviews, and social media mentions, further enhance authenticity and fosters trust among potential customers, influencing purchasing decisions and brand perception.

Additionally, customers' active participation in discussions, referrals, and online community-building efforts strengthens the microenterprise's digital footprint, facilitating long-term customer loyalty and sustained engagement. However, the extent of customer support via social media was contingent upon factors such as perceived brand value, responsiveness of the business to customer inquiries, and the effectiveness of digital engagement strategies. To optimize customer-driven support, microenterprises must cultivate an interactive and responsive social media presence, encouraging user participation through incentives, personalized interactions, and consistent content strategies. Ultimately, leveraging customer engagement as a strategic asset on social media can significantly enhance a microenterprise's market competitiveness and longterm viability.

Social media platforms significantly enhance the ability of small business owners to interact with customers in real-time, creating a dynamic and responsive communication channel that was typically unavailable through traditional marketing channels. This focused interaction was demonstrated by business owner BO E1 stating," we run occasional paid ads targeting desired demographics". The immediacy of social media facilitates direct dialogue between businesses and their customers, allowing small business owners to address inquiries, resolve issues, and respond to feedback instantaneously. This immediate response process fosters a sense of brand loyalty and trust, as customers perceive the business as more accessible and attentive to their needs. Business owner BO A1 states, "5 star ratings and outstanding reviews make all the difference to my business". The interactive nature of social media allows for a continuous exchange of information, whereby business owners can not only react to customer feedback but also proactively engage with their audience through personalized content, surveys, and promotions. This responsiveness enhances customer satisfaction, builds brand loyalty, and creates a community-driven business model. Furthermore, the datadriven insights available on social media platforms enable small business owners to track customer sentiment and adapt their offerings and communication strategies in real time, ensuring that they remain attuned to evolving consumer preferences and market trends.

The sheer volume of content, combined with increasingly aggressive algorithms, can lead to information overload, where unrelated posts or ads obscure relevant business content. The information overload reduces the effectiveness of social media as a reliable discovery tool and increases cognitive impact on consumers, who may become fatigued or frustrated when sifting through excessive, non-targeted information. Privacy concerns also pose a significant usability challenge, as consumers are wary of sharing personal information due to frequent data breaches and misuse of personal data for targeted advertising. Some of these perceptions are provided in Appendix I.

Prominent terms such as "reviews," "business," and "quality" suggest that customers prioritize timely communication and expectations in both products and interactions. Additionally, the presence of words like "comments," and "experience" underscores the significance of reputation and peer influence in shaping purchasing decisions. The recurrence of terms related to concerns, such as "service" or "engagement," highlights areas where businesses may need to improve responsiveness and problem resolution. As a qualitative analytical tool, the word cloud enables small businesses to identify key themes in customer feedback, informing strategic efforts to enhance digital engagement, brand loyalty, and overall customer satisfaction.

The word cloud in Figure 10 offers a visual representation of the most frequently occurring terms in customer responses to small business social media inquiries, providing valuable insights into consumer expectations, preferences, and engagement patterns. The word cloud denotes the perceptions and attitudes toward the use of social media to both find and use local, microenterprise type businesses. Many of the words identified in the cloud indicate use of social media, such as reviews and decisions, and values of customers such as service and products.

Figure 10

Microenterprise Customer Social Media Word Cloud

Note. Figure 10 provides a visual summary of customer perceptions (Wieland, 2025)

These usability issues collectively diminish the trust and ease-of-use that consumers expect, potentially dissuading them from engaging with businesses via social media channels. Addressing these challenges was crucial for enhancing the consumer experience, ensuring inclusivity, and fostering a more sustainable relationship between businesses and their audiences on the Microenterprises social media platform.

Chapter Summary

The recruitment process started after the Institutional Review Board approved the research, then after businesses were identified and informed consent forms were presented and signed by business owners. The interview, email instrument and online survey process was utilized for data collection, and the questions were presented and answered with the goal of capturing at least three selected responses, one from the owner, one from the employees and at least one from a customer, or user of social media from that business. The data collection was completed using a combination of ZOOM or inperson interviews, email instruments for owners and employees and SurveyMonkey surveys for customers. The email instrument was utilized in the case where ZOOM scheduling was problematic, and the interviewer did not want to interrupt the company's daily operations or where the business owner was unavailable for a ZOOM interview.

Artifacts captured during the data collection process included the following:

- Web site information capture
- Informal business follow-up visits
- Facebook social media visits

The three emergent themes from the interviews, email instruments and online survey results indicated the following:

- Theme 1: Social media is an excellent marketing medium.
- Theme 2: The technology is an easy-to-use tool for small business owners.
- Theme 3: Social media creates a greater ability for business owners to react with customers.

Chapter 4 provided a comprehensive discussion on how the data was collected and analyzed and discussed data coding and comments from participants. Chapter 4 presented themes and sub-themes derived from the data collected, resulting in emergent themes. These emergent themes provide insight into potential conclusions and recommendations. Chapter 5 provides conclusions and recommendations for social media's future use by small businesses along with recommendations for future research

and limitations of the study.

Chapter 5

Conclusions and Recommendations

The purpose of the current qualitative exploratory multiple case study was to explore the perceptions of owners, employees, and customers of family-owned microenterprises in Delaware, Maryland, and Virginia, or the DELMARVA region, regarding microenterprise owner reasons and successes for implementing social media and the challenges faced in creating successful customer-focused social media business strategies. A primary goal of the qualitative exploratory multiple case study was to understand why and how small, microenterprise owners have implemented social media marketing, perceptions of employees regarding the influence of social media and customers use of social media as technology to locate goods and services. The study also examined customer's perception on the ease-of-use on the business social media technologies and more specifically applications.

Based on the results of the data analysis, the themes that emerged followed and aligned with the research questions, which included the reasons for using social media marketing, the influence of social media on consumers and the ease or usability of the social media tools or platforms. In Chapter 5, the discussion of findings, limitations of the study and recommendations for further research are to follow.

Research Questions

The three research questions defined in Chapter 1 that provided the guide for this study:

R1: What are the owner perceptions of family-owned microenterprises in DELMARVA, more specifically the Baltimore region, regarding their reasons for implementing social media strategies? This question was crucial in understanding the motivations behind adopting social media strategies in these businesses.

R2: What are the employee perceptions of family-owned microenterprises in DELMARVA, more specifically the Baltimore region, regarding the influence of customers on business social media strategies?

R3: What are the customer perceptions of family-owned microenterprises in DELMARVA, more specifically the Baltimore region, regarding the accuracy and usability of the social media interfaces?

Discussion of Findings

The study findings are based on the three main research questions, (a) what are the owner perceptions of family-owned microenterprise in the DELMARVA region, regarding their reasons for implementing social media strategies, (b) What are the employee perceptions of family-owned microenterprises in DELMARVA, regarding the influence of customers on business social media strategies, and (c) What are the customer perceptions of family-owned microenterprises in DELMARVA, regarding the accuracy and usability of the social media interfaces. The data captured provided support the three themes through recurring ideas and interpretations of meaning. The small or microenterprise business owner expressed qualitative perceptions and experiences regarding the use of social media technologies as a marketing tool to boost a competitive advantage within each market segment.

In comparing the results from Chapter 4, with one significant result being the ease of use, against the numbers of social media platforms available, the social media technology implementation creates both opportunities and challenges for small business owners seeking to enhance their digital presence. There was one significant result being the ease of use on some social media platforms that required minimal configuration on both the users' owners and users side. The ease of social media use was a critical determinant in adoption and sustained engagement, particularly for resource-constrained enterprises. A review of 2021 literature revealed a spectrum of experiences influenced by technological literacy, perceived usefulness, and platform complexity.

Ease of Use and Digital Literacy

Alford and Page (2021) emphasized that many small business owners perceive social media as user-friendly once a baseline level of digital competence was achieved. Alford and Pages' (2021) qualitative study revealed that owners with moderate digital literacy adapt quickly, leveraging easy to use, intuitive interfaces with mobile accessibility that supports customer engagement. The quality and intuitiveness of social media applications underpins the notion that ease of use was closely tied to prior digital exposure rather than inherent platform simplicity.

In contrast, Ahmad et al. (2021) identified significant disparities in social media usability across demographic lines. Older entrepreneurs and those in rural settings report difficulty navigating newer features like stories, reels, and analytics dashboards. Older users often perceive social media tools as "labor-intensive" rather than streamlined, suggesting that perceived ease of use was contextual and influenced by prior experience, education, and support networks. In the current research, one owner had no real line of succession for the business, or plan to keep the business in the family, leading to a lack of using social media technologies to the fullest.

Technological Affordances and Platform-Specific Challenges

Nambisan et al. (2021) argued that while platforms such as Facebook and Instagram offer user-friendly interfaces, the algorithmic complexity and content performance variability often deter small business owners from feeling confident in their use. Nambisan et al.'s (2021) research indicated that ease of access does not equate to ease of effective use especially when platform algorithms are opaque and success was contingent on nuanced content strategies. During the research interviews, two subjects indicated that they knew that they were not using social media marketing to the technologies fullest potential and planned on learning more about how to use it.

Support Mechanisms and Training

The study findings emphasized that external support could mitigate perceived barriers to use. Ahmad et al. (2021) noted that government-sponsored digital literacy programs and peer mentoring dramatically improve perceptions of ease. The current study supported Ahmads et al.'s claim.

The current research study included owners and employees with varying levels of comfort with technology, where some embraced new methods of marketing using social media and some outsourced the process as a matter of business. The research included owners and employees with varying levels of comfort with technology, where some embraced new methods and marketing using social media and some outsourced the process as a matter of business. With structured guidance, even less tech-savvy microenterprise owners reported increased confidence in navigating platforms features and integrating them into business models.

Participation in the current study involved business owners, employees, and customers. This participation included Zoom meetings for business owners and employees if available, or if scheduling conflicts arose, an email instrument was utilized. The interviews and surveys consisted of seven questions for employees, and eight questions for owners. The participants answered open-ended semi-structured questions, and the survey typically lasted approximately 30 minutes. Customers were provided with links and QR codes to access questions online via SurveyMonkey. For the Zoom and online survey data analysis, NVivo and Microsoft Word applications were used. The following themes emerged from the data captured.

Theme 1: The Owner Reasons and Perceptions for Implementing Social Media

Social media serves as an unparalleled marketing medium due to its ability to reach vast and varied audiences while enabling personalized engagement. Platforms such as Facebook, Instagram, and TikTok collectively amass billions of active users, offering businesses unprecedented access to global consumers (Infante & Mardikaningsih, 2022). These platforms employ advanced algorithms to target specific demographics, optimizing campaign effectiveness and enhancing return on investment. For instance, TikTok' s innovative approach to short-form video content has reshaped how consumers discover products, with 67% of users reporting inspiration to shop from the platform (Vera et al., 2024). Additionally, social media's cost-effectiveness makes it an attractive option for businesses of all sizes, allowing even small enterprises to compete on a global scale. By integrating organic and paid strategies, marketers can cultivate brand awareness, boost customer retention, and increase conversion rates significantly.

Social media use facilitates interactive and dynamic engagement, fostering stronger customer relationships and loyalty. Businesses benefit from two-way communication, addressing inquiries and concerns in real-time, a critical aspect for 79% of consumers who expect responses within 24 hours (Wu et al., 2023). The research conducted for the current study found that all five microenterprises used all or most of the social media applications listed, that is, Facebook, Instagram, and TikTok.

There are new social media applications building on the success of the older solutions, such as Quest, Threads and Supernova. As a microenterprise owner, the importance in considering new applications and marketing methods is observed and recognized for potential use. Social media applications with the greatest marketing potential for their business type should be implemented. The most noteworthy basis for being successful is to ensure the business is on the same platforms as customers, to stay focused on where consumers are using the technology and stay alert for changes in the social media landscape.

Social media has presented significant opportunities for small businesses to provide lower costs and brand awareness; however, there are challenges with negative electronic word-of-mouth as indicated by (Wu et al., 2023). Consumer complaints can have negative consequences for the small business and must be dealt with quickly and efficiently. Social media platforms can support the resolution to customer complaints and provide the consumer with a positive perception of the small business. Conversely, if a small business owner responds negatively to a negative review, that response can have compounding negative consequences to their business, as comments on some platforms are extremely hard to remove. However, the positive possibilities for social media use are only limited by the creativity of the microenterprise owner and can build consumer loyalty and expand business possibilities.

The creative flexibility of social media platforms, supporting formats such as live streams, stories, and video posts, allows brands to captivate their audiences and adapt to trending consumer behaviors. Furthermore, these platforms provide detailed analytics, enabling marketers to fine-tune strategies based on engagement metrics, audience behavior, and conversion rates. According to the literature approximately 78% of consumers state that a brand's social media presence influences their purchasing decisions, emphasizing the medium's profound impact on consumer behavior (Vera et al., 2024). The combination of expansive reach, interactivity, and data-driven capabilities solidifies social media's role as a cornerstone of modern marketing strategies.

Theme 2: The Employee Perceptions of the Influence of Social Media Marketing

Social media technology has emerged as a user-friendly tool for the microenterprise business owners, offering intuitive platforms and features that streamline operations and enhance customer engagement. Platforms such as Facebook, Instagram, and TikTok, were heavily represented in the research that provides accessible interfaces which are designed to accommodate varying levels of technical expertise, allowing business owners to quickly establish and manage their own business digital presence. Built-in tools such as Meta's Business Suite and analytics dashboards enable efficient scheduling, posting, and performance tracking without requiring extensive training. These functionalities are particularly advantageous for small businesses with limited resources, enabling them to compete with larger competitors by leveraging targeted advertising and direct communication channels (Vera et al., 2024).

Social media technology fosters a two-way communication channel that is essential for building customer relationships and trust. Features like real-time messaging and interactive posts can support and help the microenterprise Businesses owners connect with their audience while addressing inquiries promptly (Vera et al., 2024). The ability to engage directly with customers, even after purchases are made, not only fosters loyalty but also provides valuable insights into customer preferences and behaviors, enabling tailored marketing strategies.

Additionally, social media platforms support multimedia content such as videos, infographics, and user-generated content, which are easy to create and share, further enhancing accessibility for small business owners (Abkenar et al., 2021). These considerations make social media an indispensable tool in modern small business operations. During the research, all five microenterprises were identified and implemented with some ease, and with most of the social media applications used for marketing purposes. One of the small businesses outsourced most of its social media and marketing efforts to focus on the core sales of the business. However, the ease of use for various aspects of social media, such as media sharing and status updates, as well as implementation of social media technologies was found to be consistent across all microenterprises in the research study.

One such aspect of social media included media sharing services that provided the uploading of photos, videos and status's provide insights to consumer's interest and behaviors that may be beneficial to the small business owner (Abkenar et al., 2021) and respondents indicated these activities were easy to accomplish. Most popular social networks provide simple application programing interfaces that can collect and extract data by using web requests. This information can be beneficial to the small business owner.

Theme 3: The Customer Perceptions of the Usability of Social Media Tools

Social media provides microenterprise business owners with an unparalleled ability to interact with customers, creating direct and meaningful relationships that drive engagement and loyalty. Platforms like Facebook, Instagram, and Twitter allow businesses to respond instantly to customer inquiries, feedback, and concerns, facilitating real-time interaction. This two-way communication helps build trust and fosters a sense of community among customers, which is essential for brand loyalty. By using tools like centralized inboxes or customer relationship management systems integrated into platforms such as Meta's Business Suite, businesses can ensure that no customer interaction goes unnoticed, strengthening their service responsiveness and fostering longterm customer relationships (Sreejesh et al., 2020).

Moreover, the authentic and humanized engagement made possible through social media enhances the customer experience by addressing individual needs and preferences. Customers increasingly value personalized interactions and seek authentic connections with the brands they support. Small businesses can meet these expectations by using social media to demonstrate empathy, resolve complaints quickly, and actively listen to their audience. This dynamic also allows small businesses to gather customer insights, helping them refine their offerings and marketing strategies. The growing emphasis on authenticity in social media makes these platforms ideal for creating deeper, more meaningful connections that drive customer satisfaction and loyalty (Sreejesh et al.,
2020).

Limitations

The current study research plan maintained risk analysis with respect to participant and data protection and confidentiality through the informed consent process. However, a formal risk assessment plan with respect to unforeseen issues was not included for limitations with respect to unforeseen issues that emerged during the data collecting and data analysis periods. A time limitation was identified early in the data collection stage, as business owners and employees were unable to attend ZOOM meetings, so email instruments were implemented to collect data. Additionally, there were delays in data collection connected to the end of year holidays; the timing did influence the suitability of participant interactions, but did not impact on the quality of the research data.

A limitation that was not originally considered was participants' lack of social media use. There was one employee from one of the microenterprises who did not use social media as part of their daily routine and did not interact directly with customers as they were not in a customer-facing position. Additionally, an "act of God" incident limited the study.

An unforeseen issue creating study limitations resulted from the Francis Scott Key Bridge disaster in metropolitan Baltimore, Maryland. There was a major impact felt by some businesses in the metropolitan Baltimore because of the destruction of the Francis Scott Key Bridge in Baltimore Harbor. The bridge collapse may have impacted customer numbers for some of the merchants during the study period.

Although the bridge collapse created business downturns felt by some businesses because of the destruction of the Francis Scott Key Bridge in Baltimore Harbor, it was difficult to measure the extent of the slowdown in sales. Supply chains were disrupted and traffic around the bridge collapse was rerouted, which may have influenced customer sales and business during the study period. Some businesses noted that a loss of customer traffic occurred for their stores, most specifically indicated by the merchant who encountered interruptions in the supply chain as Thanopoulou and Strandenes (2025) stated.

Other unforeseen limitations considerably altered the study exploring social media usage among small businesses in metropolitan Baltimore. Many business leaders lacked formal training or prior experience with social media technologies, which often resulted in inconsistent content strategies or underutilization of platform-specific features. The challenge of handling the social learning curve was overcome quickly by most microenterprise business owners who took part in the current research study.

Disparities in platform preferences and accessibility often limit the study ability to generalize study findings across diverse small business sectors (Pitafi et al., 2020). Most of the business owners in the current research study implemented social media applications such as Facebook business pages, and TikTok internally with minimal numbers of issues. However new and innovative social media applications such as WhatsApp, WeChat and Line are not being implemented with these microentrepreneurs, yet the applications have exciting potential for future use. Technological innovation was one area that emerged as a point in the study where microenterprise owners should pay close attention to and consider adopting new and up-and-coming technologies for use.

Market changes or technological updates during the study period had the potential for generating external disruptions that limited either the data collection or data analysis.

For instance, shifting algorithms on platforms like Facebook or Instagram can alter engagement metrics, making longitudinal comparisons difficult. Additionally, the on/off talks regarding the implementation of trade tariffs may have an impact on product availability and pricing to merchants. Market fluctuations and technical software updates may have complicated the interpretation of data, as these critical shifts introduced elements beyond a researcher's control, which potentially can distort the understanding of social media's role and its success in small business marketing (Pitafi et al., 2020).

Recommendations to Leaders and Practitioners Social media is a highly dynamic, highly influential technology that can significantly affect and benefit the small business environment (Dwivedi et al., 2021). The use of the internet and social media has modified the behavior of consumers in several ways. Consumers now view and approach product selection and services from a unique perspective. In recent years, making purchasing selections online and utilizing social media reviews from prior customers has had substantial consumer influence (Dwivedi et al., 2021). From the current study, the following recommendations were developed.

Recommendation 1: Build Social Media as Part of a Total Marketing Strategy to

Develop a Consistent Brand

The connection between the reasons and perceptions for implementing social media by the family-owned microenterprise and the small business or microenterprise owner directly aligns with the possibilities social media technology providing an excellent, easy to use marketing tool. Technology should be an amalgamation of social media and other marketing methods that include traditional forms of customer interaction. The small business normally benefits from the small-town affiliation, where the owner knows the consumer base, and markets their goods and services in traditional means such as local newspapers, flyers, and word of mouth. Nevertheless, it is important for the small business owner to understand that social media is not the panacea for solving all of the microenterprise marketing challenges.

Recommendation 2: Utilize Employees in Developing the Social Media Presence

Social media can provide the extra attention that small microenterprises need to remain competitive and react to changing consumer demands. Employees can be significant resources for the small business owner to utilize (Meske & Junglas, 2021). Social media technology does provide the ability for the microenterprise owner to remain nimble and adapt to new product opportunities given feedback from consumers captured by employees, thereby sustaining a competitive market position (Kohnová & Salajová,

2023) but is not a single solution for a complete marketing portfolio.

Recommendation 3: Engage Customers to Provide Feedback on Social Media

Trends

Customers could be the greatest form of data collection by microenterprise business owners, if only the owner engaged with customers more often. Great feedback was provided via social media applications (Marengo et al.., 2021). The tactic of capturing that feedback could be from customer surveys, consumer human interaction, word of mouth or from other customer interactions. Customers can provide data on what social media applications work well and are easy to use compared to which ones do not and what other new systems customers might be utilizing.

Actionable ideas and recommendations are provided in Table 7 with respect to the original research questions. These are suggestions and recommendations only and each business owner should evaluate what may provide value depending on the goals and objectives for each business.

Table 7

Clear and Actionable Recommendations

Research Question	Recommendations
R1 What are the owner perceptions of family-owned microenterprises in the DELMARVA region regarding their reasons for implementing social media strategies? **Theme 1** The Owner Reasons and Perceptions for Implementing Social Media – easy to use and implement – free in many cases.	Developing a Consistent Brand Narrative across platforms, which are easy to use and implement. Engage and prioritize community through social media over direct aggressive sales. Invest in authentic multimedia storytelling. The small business owner should query customers on what type of interaction works for the customer.
R2 What are the employee perceptions of family-owned microenterprises in the DELMARVA region regarding the influence of customers on business social media strategies? **Theme 2** The Employee Perceptions of the Influence of Social Media Marketing – become involved in the social media process.	Implement and follow measurable content calendar for key performance indicators that involve employees. Employees should be included in any training or content creation process. Employee perceptions and participation is important. Employees can provide significant social media support.
R3 What are the customer perceptions of family-owned microenterprises in the DELMARVA region regarding the accuracy and usability of the social media interfaces? **Theme 3** The Customer Perceptions of Usability of Social Media Tools	The business owner needs to query customers for ease of social media use and build systems and technologies that work for the customer and the business owner.

Note. Table 7 (Wieland, 2024)

The ability to remain nimble and adjust to consumer demands provides for greater competitive advantages over other likeminded businesses (Kohnová & Salajová, 2023). With the growth of online purchasing capabilities provided by companies like Amazon, eBay and just about every major store, local brand name awareness was even more important. Microenterprise business owners should be flexible and adaptable to strategic marketing changes and plan accordingly and remain open to changes in technological trends and use. The social media architecture is dynamic, fluid, and new methods of using the technologies should be a marketing strategy for all microenterprises to remain competitive.

A recommendation is that each microenterprise implement a social media strategy that provides activities across all the platforms customers of that microenterprise use. If, for example, customers of one microenterprise tend to use Facebook rather than TikTok or web services to learn of local products and service providers, then that microenterprise should focus efforts on Facebook rather than other platforms. The microenterprise owner should also be searching for new applications that could benefit and help grow the business. Platforms should be reassessed annually to ensure that the social media platforms are providing value and ensuring microenterprise owners are staying current with social media trends. An important consideration will be flexibility with an eye to new capabilities.

A noteworthy point that occurred during the research was that when using social media platforms, an owner should provide space to acknowledge

consumer problems and provide prompt solutions to those problems while maintaining a vigilant eye on conversations concerning the microenterprise brand name. Finally, the local
microenterprise should not totally disregard traditional methods of advertising, such as flyers and newspaper ads, when creating a marketing strategy, rather these forms may have less emphasis than social media marketing based in their clientele social media interactive news.

Recommendations for Future Research

The current research focused on small family-owned microenterprises, where each business had a limited number of employees, revenues were at a limited number and, of course, were family owned and operated. Further research into small businesses in the DELMARVA area that are not family owned and do not fit the microenterprise model, yet fit into the same employee and revenue constraints, could be important. These enterprises include such businesses as franchised businesses, where the owner has a limited number of employees and has a limited revenue. In this situation, the local business may be family-owned, but the authorization is granted to a local individual or group to carry out commercial activities by a core company, such as Dunkin Donuts for example. These businesses have a limited number of employees and revenue but are acting as an agent to the larger organizations, which support and may have implemented a significant social media presence (Dwivedi et al., 2021).

The expansion of research into a greater geographic area in the DELMARVA to include small businesses and offerings in Virginia and

Delaware that verify the findings applied evaluated in the Baltimore area could also be beneficial. The research can be applied to many types of small business, as social media as a marketing tool has grown globally into areas that are unrelated to direct consumer purchasing, such as online TikTok and YouTube services. These services provide additional income to high performing content providers that have large numbers of followers. There are also services that provide goods and monetary rewards to product reviewers who post content on purchase pages such as Amazon and eBay.

The services that offer goods or monetary incentives to perform product reviews can provide consumers with a method to generate content on e-commerce platforms such as Amazon and eBay. The ability to process online transactions represents a strategic intersection of consumer engagement and influence on marketing. These incentivized product reviews, while potentially amplifying visibility and perceived credibility, also raise critical considerations regarding authenticity, regulatory compliance, and the ethical implications of compensated endorsements in digital marketplaces. There are many ways that social media research can be applied and several different distinctions between offerings and circumstances.

Chapter Summary

The purpose of the current qualitative exploratory multiple case study was to explore the perceptions of owners and employees at family-owned microenterprises in the Delaware, Maryland, and Virginia, or the DELMARVA region focusing on the Baltimore Maryland area, regarding their reasons for implementing social media strategies, the success of those strategies, and the challenges faced in using those strategies. The main themes that resulted from the research were; 1. Social media is an excellent marketing medium, but should not be used as a sole marketing tool; 2. The social media technology is an easy-to-use tool for the microenterprise business owner, but the owner should also be aware of new social media applications; 3. Social media creates an increased ability for microenterprises owners to interact with customers.

The study answered the three research questions.

R1: What are the owner perceptions of family-owned microenterprises in DELMARVA, more specifically the Baltimore region, regarding their reasons for implementing social media strategies? This question was crucial in understanding the motivations behind adopting social media strategies in these businesses.

R2: What are the employee perceptions of family-owned microenterprises in DELMARVA, more specifically the Baltimore region, regarding the influence of customers on business social media strategies?

R3: What are the customer perceptions of family-owned microenterprises in DELMARVA, more specifically the Baltimore region, regarding the accuracy and usability of the social media interfaces?

Social media is ubiquitous and impactful to serious marketing efforts, by large and small business and has had a profound impact on society. The research contributes to the body of knowledge by highlighting the influence that social media has on the familyowned microenterprise business community, specifically in the highly transient

Baltimore, Maryland, region.

www.ingramcontent.com/pod-product-compliance
Lightning Source LLC
Chambersburg PA
CBHW071344230926
51846CB00002B/441
9787123733060